A Life Saver for New Teachers

Mentoring Case Studies to Navigate the Initial Years

Brandon Geuder, Richard E. Lange,
and Scott Scafidi

ROWMAN & LITTLEFIELD EDUCATION

A division of
ROWMAN & LITTLEFIELD PUBLISHERS, INC.
Lanham • New York • Toronto • Plymouth, UK

Published by Rowman & Littlefield Education
A division of Rowman & Littlefield Publishers, Inc.
A wholly owned subsidary of The Rowman & Littlefield Publishing Group, Inc.
4501 Forbes Boulevard, Suite 200, Lanham, Maryland 20706
http://www.rowmaneducation.com

Estover Road, Plymouth PL6 7PY, United Kingdom

British Library Cataloguing in Publication Information Available

Library of Congress Cataloging-in-Publication Data
Geuder, Brandon.
  A life saver for new teachers : mentoring case studies to navigate the initial years /
Brandon Geuder, Richard E. Lange, and Scott Scafidi.
    p. cm.
  ISBN 978-1-61048-375-9 (cloth : alk. paper) — ISBN 978-1-61048-377-3 (electronic)
  1. First year teachers—United States. 2. Teachers—Training of—United States.
3. Mentoring in education—United States. 4. Teacher effectiveness—United States.
I. Lange, Richard E. II. Scafidi, Scott. III. Title.
  LB2844.1.N4G48 2010
  371.1—dc22   2011003617

♾TM The paper used in this publication meets the minimum requirements of American National Standard for Information Sciences—Permanence of Paper for Printed Library Materials, ANSI/NISO Z39.48-1992.

Printed in the United States of America

Contents

Preface   v
Brian Patrick Roach

Foreword   vii
Bobb Darnell

1   Whose Job Is It Anyway? Defining the Roles of the
Mentor and New Teacher   1
Data Analysis by Bradley Wadle, Northwestern University

2   So What's the Point? Some Commonsense Solutions   21

3   How Can We Make This Work? Mentors Overcoming
Obstacles   31

4   Isn't My Mentor Supposed to Help Me? When Mentors
and New Teachers Struggle to Connect with Each Other   53

About the Authors   97

Preface

Brian Patrick Roach

New teachers need support. From having problems with the cooperating teacher to discovering bruises on a student, new teachers do not have the knowledge or wisdom to take effective action. The same, unfortunately, can be said of cooperating teachers and mentors. With more than sixty authentic teaching and mentoring scenarios, each with recommended solutions, this book provides the practical support that new teachers, cooperating teachers, and mentors need.

Chapter 1, *Whose Job Is It Anyway? Defining the Roles of the Mentor and New Teacher*, has ten scenarios. At the end of each scenario, there are teacher-recommended solutions—from two distinct groups of teachers: experienced (30+ years) and new teacher (0–6 years), a Likert scale (to reflect upon the action plans), and a space for writing notes and comments.

Chapter 2, *So What's the Point? Some Commonsense Solutions*, is a rapid set of twenty-five mini-scenarios ranging from the situation of "Before the winter holiday break you receive gifts from students. Where would you find the students' addresses to write thank-you notes?" to "After school while cleaning up the classroom, you discover an anonymously written note in which one student explains thoughts of suicidal ideation to another student." These actual teaching occurrences shed light on the disparities of education and provide the reader with relevant brainstorming opportunities.

Chapter 3, *How Can We Make This Work? Mentors Overcoming Obstacles*, presents twenty scenarios that are more detailed than those in chapter 1. The premise is that the cooperating teacher is well trained and ready to help, but the new teacher is causing difficulties. Consequently, the mentor needs to intervene and resolve the issue(s).

Chapter 4, *Isn't My Mentor Supposed to Help Me? When Mentors and New Teachers Struggle to Connect with Each Other*, contains ten in-depth case studies that seem to be overlooked by teacher induction programs. Each case study tells of unique circumstances where the new teacher is working well but the cooperating teacher is not. Four thought-provoking questions and further analysis follow each scenario.

This book wants an interactive reader. It wants the reader to brainstorm a resolution process: first, to identify the issue(s); second, to consider resources to use for the creation of potential solutions for the issue(s); and third, to construct a solution to mend the issue(s). For the teacher or mentor who is looking for a preparation book that is immediately applicable to education, this book is it—it serves practicality.

I am a new teacher, and I could have used this book before my practicum. It could have kick-started my experience by requiring me to brainstorm about potential teaching scenarios that I might encounter, such as having a gifted student in class. This book is a testament to new teachers' need of support; the scenarios exist because support did not. New teachers can refresh education with innovative ideas and invigorating personalities, but such a summer breeze quickly stills without the wind at its back.

—Brian Patrick Roach

Foreword

Bobb Darnell, president, Achievement Strategies, Inc.

Just in time! The exciting book *A Life Saver for New Teachers: Mentoring Case Studies to Navigate the Initial Years,* has arrived with exactly what these changing times in education need. Changes in accountability to provide equitable achievement for all students and expectations to prepare for twenty-first century competencies and higher-level thinking skills are dramatically challenging schools.

Along with these demands, students, family structures, resources, and teachers are changing. The baby boomers are retiring en masse, and new teachers are filling the gaps with youth and inexperience. The twenty-something teachers bring different styles, characteristics, and needs that may clash with veteran teachers and high achievement expectations.

Teaching is difficult today for early-career teachers, and the dropout rate of new teachers is high in urban schools, which have the most difficulty both attracting and then retaining fully certified teachers. The need for mentoring new teachers is high, and induction of new teachers can take three to five years. But, there is no time to waste. The teaching skills needed to handle a very fluid, fast-paced information revolution must be nurtured effectively and efficiently to assure equitable learning opportunities and high achievement for students.

Schools need the best ways to make new teachers feel confident, welcome, connected to others, supported, and successful, and this useful book is an innovative approach designed to support new teachers and develop internal teacher leadership capacity. *A Life Saver for New Teachers* provides new teachers and their mentors with practical, commonsense scenarios and case studies to apply reflection and interaction skills about teaching and learning.

The authors offer years of experience to guide mentors and new teachers as they define and implement their roles. More than fifty engaging, real-life educational scenarios and case studies provide the impetus for the problem solving, decision making, and planning teachers need to address daily occurrences in classrooms and other school contexts. While the authors put an emphasis on the discovery process and teacher-mentor interactions and relationships, they offer solutions and options based upon a blend of research and tested practice.

Yes, *A Life Saver for New Teachers* is here just in time. It truly represents an engaging and effective way to provide both mentors and new teachers with the professional learning opportunities to address the changing faces of education today. With this book everybody wins. New and veteran teachers hone their skills and acquire just-in-time knowledge. Students get a guarantee of effective classroom teachers and a chance for high achievement. Parents develop and sustain greater support and appreciation for schools. And, society will have contributing citizens who are capable of competing in the world economy by using their knowledge, creativity, and higher-level thinking skills.

CHAPTER 1

Whose Job Is It Anyway?

DEFINING THE ROLES OF THE MENTOR AND NEW TEACHER

Data Analysis by Bradley Wadle

How to Use This Chapter

Whether a teacher is brand-new to the profession or new to a school district, this book has been designed to help teachers make thoughtful decisions. This text is intended to help establish a working relationship between mentors and new teachers by providing a forum for various school-related situations to be pondered, discussed, and resolved. It will help new teachers become more familiar with resources that the school has available as they journey through their first years of teaching. It gives mentors an avenue for discussing topics that affect new teachers every day.

After reading each scenario, teachers should consider the following:

1) What are the key issues in this scenario?
2) Which resource and/or person would you use to find a solution?
   Think of other school personnel besides your mentor. In some cases, you or a fellow new teacher may offer the best solution.
3) What action plan can I put in place to resolve the issues?

Teachers should read each item carefully and respond by using the three-step process outlined above. Many scenarios seem straightforward, but taking the time to look deeper at them will yield interesting observations about the many ethical, social, and emotional aspects of teaching. This process can be done individually, in a group, or one-on-one with a mentor.

After completing each scenario, teachers should reflect upon their solutions. The reflection scale below gives teachers the opportunity to critically evaluate their decision making.

Reflect

How comfortable do you feel about your action plans?				
Uncertain		Good		Confident
1	2	3	4	5

Reflection upon your decisions is an extremely important part of the process as it is both an end and a beginning. If uncertainty about an action plan is present, reevaluate the decisions, do some research, speak to new people, and begin the process anew.

Analysis of Scenarios

Depending on the context in which you work and who you are, each of this chapter's scenarios can have different answers. To that end, the analysis provided after each scenario should not be thought of as "correct" or "valid." Instead, it is an example from our research that may illuminate your thinking, and it is provided to give you an idea of the diverse answers that are possible when confronted with these scenarios.

The ten scenarios in this chapter were selected to be a part of an online survey hosted by the Mentoring Leadership and Resource Network's website: www.mentors.net.

Respondents were asked to identify how many years of teaching experience they had. We then disaggregated the data into two groups: teachers with six years or less of teaching experience and those with thirty years or more. Responses to the three questions posed after each of the ten scenarios were then analyzed.

For our research purposes, we defined new teachers as those with 0–6 years of experience. Experienced teachers have 30+ years of experience. While some of the new teachers answered many of the questions in a similar fashion to the more experienced teachers, there were clearly some who offered different solutions in terms of whom they would go to as well as what kind of action plan they would create.

The unique qualities of the varied replies offer a great deal of insight as you wrestle with these scenarios. These replies are provided for you after each scenario under the heading, *What Did Other Teachers Think?* As you read, ask yourself these questions: Why was the response given? Is the response helpful, or does it concern you? What similarities and differences exist between your responses and those listed below?

Scenarios

Scenario 1. You are planning an instructional activity that requires more space. How would you find out if the gymnasium will be available during the time you would like to use it for a special class event?

What is the key issue in this scenario?
Which resource and/or person would you use to find a solution?
Create an action plan to resolve the situation.

What Did Other Teachers Think?

Resources	Action Plans
—PE Teacher —Principal —Secretary —Unspecified "Person in Charge"	—Compromise with other teachers to use the space —Check scheduling procedures —Seek alternate spaces as a backup plan —Modify the activity to take place in the room

The new-teacher group chose, far and away, the PE teacher as the most likely person to contact about scheduling the gym. The next most frequent response was to ask the principal. Some new teachers would approach the secretary, and a small group would contact "the person responsible" or "the person in charge." This last response could be seen either as uncertainty about which person that is, or perhaps as an acknowledgment that every school may have a different person responsible for scheduling large spaces.

One person suggested compromising with other teachers, seeming to indicate that all teachers had some time in the gymnasium during a school week. A small number of respondents in this group indicated that they would need to check procedures for using a space like the gym, and some even had backup plans: either they would look into alternate spaces (the cafeteria, the auditorium, outside), or they would modify their plans to allow the activity to occur in their own classroom.

At first glance, there is not much difference in how the 30+ group responded. Most experienced teachers would ask the PE teacher. Some would go to the principal or to the secretary, and a few mentioned "the person in charge." The experienced teachers were more likely to check the school event calendar directly and less likely to inquire about exact procedures.

Like the 0–6 group, experienced teachers would make backup plans; close to the same number mentioned using alternate spaces or modifying their plans if no large spaces were available. Perhaps the biggest difference is that respondents in the 30+ group were more likely to describe their plan and explain why they needed the larger space to whomever they were requesting it from.

Scenario 2. You notice small bruises on the arms of one of your students.

What is the key issue in this scenario?
Which resource and/or person would you use to find a solution?
Create an action plan to resolve the situation.

What Did Other Teachers Think?

Key Issues	Resources	Action Plans
—Possibility of child abuse —Responsibility to report —General health and well-being of student	—Student w/bruises —Guidance Counselor —Social Worker —School Nurse —Principal —Student's Parents —Outside Resource	—Document observations —Continue monitoring the student —Contact outside resources (i.e., Department of Family and Child Services) —Arrange a meeting with the student and an administrator or social worker —Arrange a meeting with parents/call the parents —Talk to other students to learn background information about the home

It is no surprise that this scenario brought about a great deal of concern among both groups about the possibility of child abuse, and both groups showed an awareness of a teacher's responsibility to report suspected child abuse.

Talking to both the student and a guidance counselor or social worker were the most common courses of action for respondents in the new-teacher group. The school nurse and the principal were also mentioned often. The parents of the child would also be consulted, but much less frequently.

One respondent stated that she or he would talk to other students. The 0–6 group was more likely than the experienced group to document their observations, and many specifically stated that they would continue observing the child for further signs of abuse.

Though some respondents did mention the possibility of contacting an outside agency such as DCFS (Department of Child and Family

Services) or CPS (Child Protective Services) to report the abuse, all but one of these respondents also stated that they would discuss the matter with the student, school administration, and/or the school social worker to determine whether such action was warranted. One respondent would both talk to the student and file a report with an outside agency but did not specify if the report was contingent upon the result of the conversation with the student.

Trends among the 30+ group were similar: the counselor or social worker was the top contact, followed by the nurse, and then the principal or other administrator. Interestingly, only one respondent in the experienced teacher group stated that he or she would talk to the student's parents.

The 30+ group was also less likely to talk to the student. Two respondents in the 30+ group specifically stated that they would not speak to the student about their suspicions under any circumstances. As with the 0–6 group, some experienced teachers stated that they would contact an outside agency.

One experienced teacher listed an outside agency as the sole response to this scenario. That respondent made no mention of talking to anyone else.

Reflect

How comfortable do you feel about your action plans?				
Uncertain		Good		Confident
1	2	3	4	5

COMMENTS/NOTES:

Scenario 3. You just completed your first principal observation and did not agree with the evaluation component.

What is the key issue in this scenario?
Which resource and/or person would you use to find a solution?
Create an action plan to resolve the situation.

What Did Other Teachers Think?

Key Issues	Resources	Action Plans
—Differences in perception —How to revise the evaluation	—Teachers' Union —Principal	—Contact the teachers' union —Review teacher contract evaluation guidelines —Submit written statement specifying objections —Add comments before signing the evaluation —Discuss difference with the principal —Take suggestions and improve classroom practice —Suggest changes to evaluation process

New teachers were much more likely to focus on improving their own practice than the 30+ group. They would still talk to the evaluator and other staff members to try to get to the root of the disagreement, but many respondents from the 0–6 group mentioned something about seeing what they could do to improve for next time.

It was not always clear if this was related to improving as teachers, or just improving in the sense of getting a better evaluation. Only a few respondents from the 30+ group mentioned trying to improve.

The experienced teachers focused more on specific grievance procedures. The 30+ group was much more likely to contact the union, review the contract evaluation guidelines, follow specific grievance procedures (most notably, add comments to the evaluation before signing it), and submit a written statement specifying objections to the supervisor's evaluation. Many of the respondents in the 30+ group mentioned grievance procedures; few respondents from the 0–6 group did so.

The 0–6 group was slightly more likely to suggest changing the evaluation process. Could this be because the 30+ group knows that the evaluation process is determined by the teacher contract, not by the whim of the principal, and that changing the process requires committees, meetings, and union votes?

Scenario 4. As coach of the basketball team, you receive a number of phone calls from parents who feel that their children are not getting enough "game time." Immediately after the next basketball game, you are confronted by several hostile parents.

What is the key issue in this scenario?
Which resource and/or person would you use to find a solution?
Create an action plan to resolve the situation.

What Did Other Teachers Think?

Key Issues	Resources	Action Plans
—Wrong time for confrontation —Aggressive behavior of parents	—Parents	—Parent meeting at a later date —Call for security or police —Accommodate parents by discussing player performance; review game tapes —Give kids more playing time —Draft a game plan that includes all players —Discuss team philosophy —Check for district policies on playing time and adhere to those rules —Develop a parent conduct contract —Give parents the ability to vote on team focus: winning or equal playing time

Most of the respondents agreed that right after the game was not the place for a discussion to happen, and that a meeting, either with individual parents or all parents together, should be held at a later time. A couple of teachers in the 0–6 group, perhaps somewhat tongue in cheek, stated that they would run away and call the police.

Respondents in the 0–6 group seemed more likely to try to accommodate the parents, either by reviewing game tapes to see if there was any merit to the complaint, drafting a game plan to be shared with players and parents which would allow everyone to play, or simply give the kids more playing time.

Only a few in the 30+ group chose one of the above options. Only one respondent in the 30+ group would give more playing time, but only if students met a set of playing standards and adhered to a published practice schedule to reach those standards.

Several respondents in both groups stated that they would attempt to explain the playing time and coaching philosophy to the parents. Interestingly, this seemed to break down into two possible philosophies: the goal is to win, and the best players get the most playing time; or the goal is for everyone to get a chance, and winning is secondary.

In the 0–6 group, some respondents specifically stated which philosophy they followed; most leaned toward winning. The most vocal in this regard stated, "This is high school, not little league!" In the 30+ group, a few respondents specifically addressed these two philosophies but stated that the school/district needed to make clear which philosophy it followed at the beginning of the season.

One of these respondents seemed open to allowing the parents to vote to switch the team's focus but would resign as a coach if she or he did not agree with the vote. This respondent did not state to which philosophy she or he actually adheres.

A small number of respondents in the 30+ group also felt that this sort of behavior on the part of parents should not be tolerated (it can be presumed that the respondents from the 0–6 group who would run away and call the police agree).

One experienced teacher would have the parents sign a code of conduct and would not allow any student to play at all if the parents violated that agreement. Another would address the matter with parent groups.

Reflect

How comfortable do you feel about your action plans?				
Uncertain		Good		Confident
1	2	3	4	5

COMMENTS/NOTES:

Scenario 5. You feel as though you are not getting along with your mentor because there is a great deal of conflict between you two.

What is the key issue in this scenario?
Which resource and/or person would you use to find a solution?
Create an action plan to resolve the situation.

What Did Other Teachers Think?

Resources	Resources

—Mentoring Teacher
—Principal
—Department Head
  (or appropriate
  supervisor)
	—Discuss feelings with the mentoring teacher
	  and/or an administrator
	—Ask for a new mentor
	—Discuss changes to the mentoring program

The 30+ group was much more likely to go into lengthy detail about how they would go about trying to resolve the issue with their mentor or get a new one, but once the extra procedural details were boiled down, there was not much difference in the two groups about the three basic solutions: either (A) get a new mentor, (B) try to resolve issues with the current mentor, or (C) try to resolve issues and then get a new mentor if no compromise can be reached.

In the 0–6 group, few respondents went with option A, most chose option B, and some chose option C. In the 30+ group, few chose option A. Most chose options B and C, with option B receiving just a few more responses than C.

One interesting note: In talking about which resource/person to use, both groups mentioned administrators, supervisors, and the mentor program itself; however, one experienced teacher specifically stated that the mentor program should have a designated contact person to help resolve mentor/mentee problems, and that this person should not be a principal, supervisor, department chair, or anyone else responsible for evaluating teacher performance.

Scenario 6. A mother informs you that her child is not being challenged in class. She believes that the student should receive more advanced work or be placed in a more advanced class.

What is the key issue in this scenario?
Which resource and/or person would you use to find a solution?
Create an action plan to resolve the situation.

What Did Other Teachers Think?

Key Issues	Resources	Action Plans
—Mother's perception is inaccurate —Student is not challenged	—Principal —Guidance Counselor —Other teachers —Specialist teachers (i.e., gifted, honors)	—Arrange a meeting with parents and an administrator or guidance counselor —Collect data on student's previous achievement —Change placement, of the student (i.e., pull out group, gifted classroom) —Change classroom instruction for the student

The 0–6 group was more likely to identify the mother as the problem—either her perception that the child was not being challenged, or, in the most extreme case, that she was bullying the teacher. Many mentioned the mother as the main issue, compared to just a few in the 30+ group (the most extreme here mentioned "overzealous parental intrusion"). Most of the responses from both groups were more mild than the extremes—mostly "mom is concerned" or "mom thinks her child is not being challenged."

For those who thought that the mother was right, and that the child was not being properly challenged, the 30+ group was more likely to specifically put the burden on the teacher and classroom instruction by mentioning differentiation, instructional techniques, or appropriate classroom materials. The 0–6 group was more likely to simply say that the "child isn't challenged" without referencing differentiation or other instructional techniques.

Both groups turned to "administrators" roughly equally; however, when broken down further, something interesting happened: In the 0–6 group, most respondents said that they would go to the principal or their department head, while only a few mentioned going to the guidance counselor. In the 30+ group, this trend was reversed; most would seek out the guidance counselor, while only a few mentioned an administrator.

The 0–6 group was more likely to mention some sort of solution that would keep students in the current classroom, either adjusting instruction to offer more challenges, providing extra work, or promoting the child to a tutor/helper. There were many responses in the 0–6 group that suggested a placement solution—either move the child to a new classroom (but only after determining that this would be appropriate) or, in one case, to enroll the child in a pull-out program.

The 30+ group kept their options open—some of them mentioned that either a classroom solution (modifying instruction) or a placement solution (go to a more advanced class) might be appropriate, but that the case would have to be looked at first.

Only a few mentioned a placement solution without mentioning that modifying classroom instruction would be an option, and a handful mentioned a classroom instruction solution without suggesting that a placement solution would also be a possibility.

Nobody in the 0–6 group mentioned both possibilities. If they mentioned either a placement solution or an instructional solution, they did not acknowledge the other as a possibility.

Reflect

How comfortable do you feel about your action plans?				
Uncertain		Good		Confident
1	2	3	4	5

COMMENTS/NOTES:

Scenario 7. After reading the description for the next in-service program, you realize that the topic has little to do with your current teaching position. You feel you can learn more by visiting another school district that has a program similar to yours and is more suited to meeting your needs.

What is the key issue in this scenario?
Which resource and/or person would you use to find a solution?
Create an action plan to resolve the situation.

What Did Other Teachers Think?

Resources	Action Plans
—Documents about the activity (i.e., programs, pamphlets, website)	—Provide background information about the activity —Volunteer to report back on the activity
—Other teachers —Principal	—Ask the principal, but expect a "no" and make the best of it —Find other teachers to go along—strength in numbers —Suggest changes to the professional development system

The primary difference between the groups in regard to this particular scenario seems to be that the respondents of the 30+ group are savvier bargainers. The 30+ group was slightly more likely to support their request to attend a different school/district's in-service program by supplying documentation: programs, literature, agendas, anything that could help establish the value of the alternate program.

The 30+ group was also more likely to offer an additional incentive; they would report back what they found at the other in-service program either in writing or by offering a training session to their own staff. Still, despite the somewhat more sophisticated bargaining techniques, only a couple of the respondents from the 30+ acknowledged that they would actually ask for permission. They fully expected "no" as the answer. One respondent put this rather succinctly: "Make the best use of your time when permission is denied."

This is not to say that the 0–6 group were bad bargainers. Many stated that they would supply documentation of the proposed alternative, and one offered a bargaining tactic not struck upon by the 30+ group: try to find other teachers who were interested in the other in-service program, and then see if a strength-in-numbers approach would bear fruit.

A few respondents in both groups mentioned trying to address the problem by modifying the professional development system itself. A couple in the 0–6 group also proposed making modifications to the in-service provided without changing the system as a whole.

Scenario 8. You receive a new student from another country. The child rarely speaks, and the student's pronunciation of English is exceedingly difficult to understand.

What is the key issue in this scenario?
Which resource and/or person would you use to find a solution?
Create an action plan to resolve the situation.

What Did Other Teachers Think?

Key Issues	Resources	Action Plans
—Lack of teacher training —Student's language	—ESL/ELL resource or teacher —Student helpers	—Specifically indentify the student's native language —Differentiate teaching materials —Differentiate classroom practice —Change placement of student to a bilingual classroom —Learn the basics of the student's language —Use the opportunity to teach the class about new cultures —Make extra efforts to improve the comfort of the classroom

This is a scenario which is increasingly common in American schools, and a number of the respondents mentioned that they have had similar experiences or have had ESL/ELL training themselves. Most of the respondents seemed aware that the student's native language could be any language at all, and they always referred to "the student's language" generically. Only one new teacher assumed that the student's language was Spanish—certainly a possibility, but not dictated by the scenario as written.

Most teachers in both groups would contact some manner of ESL/ELL resource in their school. They would also try to find extra resources (tapes, online resources) and make use of extra visual aids in the classroom, arrange for one-on-one tutoring, and use student help-ers or "buddies" to assist the student, preferably "buddies" who spoke the student's native language. In all of these ways, the two response groups were remarkably similar.

The 0–6 group was more likely to respond that the child's English proficiency should be tested, and a few respondents in the 0–6 group suggested that the student should be moved to a bilingual classroom.

The 30+ group was much more likely to take extra efforts to make the student feel comfortable in the classroom. Some experienced teachers specifically mentioned taking steps with the express goal of providing a more comfortable, relaxed classroom atmosphere; a couple stated that they would use the situation as an opportunity to teach the class as a whole about different cultures; and one stated that she or he would make an effort to learn at least a few words in the student's native language. There were no respondents in the 0–6 group who mentioned any of these alternatives.

Reflect

How comfortable do you feel about your action plans?				
Uncertain		Good		Confident
1	2	3	4	5

COMMENTS/NOTES:

Scenario 9. Disgruntled parents claim that you have been treating their child unfairly, and as a result of your discriminatory behavior, they will be going to the administration.

What is the key issue in this scenario?
Which resource and/or person would you use to find a solution?
Create an action plan to resolve the situation.

What Did Other Teachers Think?

Resources	Action Plans
—Administrator —Parents	—Meeting with parents and administrator —Meeting with parents alone —Discuss teaching practices with the parents (defend practice) —Document classroom observations and bring them to the meeting —Reflect on personal practice and consider if parents' complaints have merit

The primary tactic among both groups seemed to be to talk to an administrator first (at least to give a heads-up), and then to arrange a meeting with the parents and an administrator both present. In both groups, about twice as many respondents seemed to be focusing on listening to the parents and trying to come to some manner of resolution than simply explaining why their actions were justified and fair.

The 30+ group seemed to approach this scenario a little bit more cautiously than the 0–6 group. Some respondents in this group stated that they would bring documentation of their actions to the meeting with the parents or administrators, while only a few from the 0–6 group did. Also, and perhaps more strikingly, only a handful of respondents from the 30+ group were willing to meet with the parents without an administrator present; many of the respondents from the 0–6 group were willing to do so.

New teachers were more likely to meet with the student to try to discuss the problem. Another interesting point is that a few respondents in the 0–6 group claimed that they would reflect on their teaching or check their own records to see whether the parents' complaint had any merit.

While both groups were more likely to approach the meeting with the goal of reaching some sort of mutually satisfactory resolution (rather than just defending themselves), this was the only direct acknowledgment from either group that the teacher might possibly be in the wrong in this scenario.

Scenario 10. A child asks you for a cup of water so he can take some aspirin that his mother gave him that morning. He says he had a headache when he left the house.

What is the key issue in this scenario?
Which resource and/or person would you use to find a solution?
Create an action plan to resolve the situation.

What Did Other Teachers Think?

Key Issues	Resources	Action Plans
—Parent gave medication to child to take on his or her own —Child's health —Legality of letting the student take medication without the school nurse's approval	—School nurse —Parents —Student medical files	—Send the student directly to the school nurse —Call home to the parents —Confiscate the aspirin —Check files for medication approval —Explore possibility of student drug use —Give the student some water to take the aspirin

There was very little difference in the two groups for this particular scenario. Both groups are well aware that only the nurse can dispense medicine (even aspirin), and nearly all said that they would send the student to the nurse.

The largest differences appear when considering whether to let the nurse call the student's parents or to call home oneself, whether to confiscate the aspirin, and whether to check the student's records to see if there is some manner of permission on file.

New teachers were somewhat more likely to let the nurse handle calling home to mom and dad, though many respondents did say they would contact the parents themselves. Though it can be inferred that many of the school policies regarding the taking of medicine stem from concerns about possible drug use on the part of students (some respondents said they would take the aspirin away from the student before sending the student to the nurse), only a few respondents specifically mentioned this.

One respondent suggested that perhaps the student merely wanted attention, and that is why he or she claimed to have a headache. Another apparently was not concerned at all about possible liability or drug issues; this teacher would allow the student to take the medication, but would give the student a new aspirin.

The 30+ group was more likely to check into the student's records to see if there was a permission form of some kind from the parent to allow the student to take aspirin at school. Some respondents said that they would call home, mostly to inform parents of school policies regarding medicine in school.

There was a subtext of concern regarding possible illicit drug use in many of the responses; as with the 0–6 group, only a few respondents voiced this concern directly. Perhaps somewhat surprising is that fewer respondents in the 30+ group said that they would take the aspirin away from the student, though one teacher would put the aspirin in a sealed envelope before sending the student to the nurse.

One teacher said that no action plan was necessary for this scenario. It is unclear whether that means that the teacher would just let the student have the aspirin, or if the teacher would send the student to the nurse and be done with the situation.

Reflect

How comfortable do you feel about your action plans?				
Uncertain		Good		Confident
1	2	3	4	5

COMMENTS/NOTES:

CHAPTER 2

So What's the Point?
SOME COMMONSENSE SOLUTIONS

How to Use This Chapter

While chapter 1 provides extended discussion of each scenario, this chapter asks you to take a look at twenty-five scenarios and determine which approach you would take to resolve the situation.

These scenarios are divided into seven categories that basically answer the question "What is the key issue?" The seven key issue categories deal with administrative personnel, management skills, parent involvement, self-confidence, money, fellow staff members, and students.

While many may find the key issue to be rather obvious, our research in chapter 1 shows that educators' responses can vary based on the following contextual differences: the school setting in which the teacher works (urban, rural, or suburban), the experience level of the teacher, the state's regulations, and so forth.

The identification of the key issue can also change from year to year based on a number of factors within a school. For instance, a new principal could enact policies that change the key issues in a scenario.

We challenge you to take a look at each scenario and see if you agree that the key issue has been properly categorized. After that, you can proceed to determine which resource and/or person you would

21

use to find a solution. Finally, create a specific action plan to resolve the situation.

You will find at the back of this chapter some answers to each scenario. These answers only provided possibilities; your decisions may vary according to a variety of factors. We have provided reasonable, if not plausible, solutions to give you food for thought. These answers may, in fact, match yours.

A word of caution—we recommend that you write down the list of resources that you would use and create an action plan for each scenario before you look at the answers. This way you are not influenced by the answers before you begin your thought process.

Scenarios

ADMINISTRATIVE PERSONNEL

1. After loading some free software on your school computer, you begin to notice a virus appearing on the screen. It gets worse as the week continues.
2. You would like to go to a board of education meeting to inform the board that class sizes are too large.
3. Because you are getting behind on your classroom work, you would like to come in on a Saturday morning and get a lot accomplished with no one around. You're not sure about getting a key for the front door or how to deal with the security alarm system.

MANAGEMENT SKILLS

4. You jam the photocopy machine and have no idea how to fix it.
5. Before the winter holiday break you receive gifts from students. Where would you find the students' addresses to write thank-you notes?

6. The district staff developer has e-mailed you information regarding an upcoming workshop being offered at a nearby location. Are you expected to attend?

PARENT INVOLVEMENT

7. A set of divorced parents has asked to have two separate parent-conferences about their child's progress.
8. Two parents have volunteered to come to your class to be guest speakers about a topic you're not too sure is appropriate for the students. Based on previous conversations with them, you're also not sure about their ability to relate to younger children.
9. During a second-grade parent-teacher conference, you explain to a child's mother that the child is displaying learning and behavioral difficulties. The mother indicates to you that she talked to the principal last year and requested that her child be retained. You soon realize that the student should have been placed in third grade.

SELF-CONFIDENCE

10. It is the middle of October, and you realize that you have parent-teacher conferences, end of the grading period, a special education report due, and open house within the next two weeks. Your coping skills are running quite thin.
11. You want to experiment with a new teaching method, but you are not sure if it will go over well with the students.
12. You feel isolated, and you believe that other staff members are giving you the cold shoulder.
13. You feel that you are not really cut out for teaching. You may want to confide these thoughts and seek a new direction.

MONEY

14. You look over your first paycheck and feel it is incorrect. Not only does your base salary seem lower than you thought, but there was no deduction for family coverage insurance.
15. In order to save some of your salary for retirement, you would like to know what the difference is between a 401(k) and a 403(b) tax-shelter program, and how to apply for such a program.
16. It is time to plan a field trip, but you're not sure about the costs of the bus, the number of chaperones needed, and how to go about collecting money from the students.
17. You would like to join a few professional education organizations. You want to know if the district will pay for the memberships and what forms need to be completed.
18. After attending an off-campus workshop, you would like to know if the school will reimburse you for some, if not all, of the expenses.

FELLOW STAFF MEMBERS

19. You feel that another teacher is harassing you and making unwelcome advances.
20. The local teachers' union is looking to gain support in its upcoming bargaining session. You are not comfortable dealing with union issues.
21. Another teacher is angry with you because he or she does not feel that you are adequately modifying a student's educational program according to the student's IEP (individualized education plan).
22. You feel as though your team/department is divided into various cliques, each with its own agenda. You try to remain neutral; however, you know any decision you make will isolate one or more of these groups.

STUDENTS

23. After school while cleaning up the classroom, you discover an anonymously written note in which one student explains thoughts of suicidal ideation to another student. You do not know for whom the note was intended.
24. You repeatedly clash with one particular student throughout a week.
25. After the administration of a standardized state test, one student informs you that a child in class cheated on the examination.

Some Suggestions and Solutions

The following answers and action plans correspond to the twenty-five scenarios in this chapter. The first response, A, answers the question, "Which resource and/or person would you use to find a solution?" The second response, B, gives a suggested action plan.

ADMINISTRATIVE PERSONNEL

1A. Contact the school or district technology personnel.
1B. Don't try to fix it yourself. If possible, send an e-mail to the IT department explaining what you did. Attach any error message that appears on your screen to give some clues as to the nature of the problem.
2A. Ask your mentor if this is an appropriate activity to take as a classroom teacher.
2B. Check the school district policy on class size. The board may say that they are within guidelines for the size of your class. Check also with appropriate union leaders.
3A. Ask the building principal as well as the maintenance staff about entering the building during off hours.

3B. Really think this one out if you feel you need to work in the building or can accomplish what you need to do at home. Perhaps arriving earlier and staying later at school may be easier, and safer, than coming in after hours.

ADMINISTRATIVE NEEDS

4A. Contact the school secretary.

4B. After trying unsuccessfully to unjam the copy machine yourself, leave the machine alone and place a note on the jammed machine that help is on the way. Ask the school secretary to call the repair person. Most schools have contracts with outside vendors to fix machines since most are leased to schools.

5A. Ask in the school office to see a list of student names or go online at the school district's internal (staff only) website address book.

5B. After securing the addresses, make sure you address the thank-you notes with the appropriate header. Not all students live with Mr. and Mrs. Smith. Names may be different; students may have only one parent.

6A. Ask your mentor what the protocol is for responding to such a flyer placed in your box.

6B. Decide first if you are interested in attending this worship. If so, contact the person who gave you the workshop brochure about how to register. Ask about securing a substitute teacher for the day and who pays the costs to attend. If you decide you do not want to attend, ask your mentor if that is acceptable. Just because the brochure was placed in your mailbox doesn't necessarily mean that you must attend the event.

PARENT ISSUES

7A. Ask your mentor and/or principal if you should duplicate the parent-teacher conference for each parent.

7B. Ask what the school district policy is. Many tell the teachers and parents that there is only one conference per child, not per adult. Explain that you'll be happy to meet with one of the parents and perhaps record the conference so the other person can hear the conversation.

8A. Contact your mentor and/or principal for advice.

8B. If you decide that it is best not to have the parent volunteers come to your class to make a presentation, thank them for their offer, but kindly inform them that their presentation topic does not align with the state curriculum standards.

9A. Look through the child's records/documents to see about previous placements in the other school. Also, contact the principal and/or special education administrator.

9B. Since it is the role of the principal to make all grade placements for students, present him or her with documents indicating that the child may have been placed in the wrong grade. Then let the principal, with suggestions from the special education director, decide what placement is appropriate for the child.

SELF-CONFIDENCE

10A. Contact your mentor, or, perhaps, a good friend who is a teacher outside of the school district.

10B. Make a priority list of what needs to be accomplished during set deadlines and how significant each thing is. Then sit down with your mentor or friend to help you get a good picture of your situation and ask for advice about how to tackle each day, one day at a time.

11A. Ask to speak with your mentor, another teacher, or department chair.

11B. Write out a detailed lesson plan of your new method of teaching and run it by other school staff members to get their ideas about your project. They may even help you in the classroom while you teach so that you have a successful experience.

12A. Contact your mentor or the director of the new-teacher induction program.

12B. Take a close look at how you relate with other staff members. Offer to share related curriculum materials to break the ice when starting a conversation. It may be that everyone is just so busy that they seem to be distant.

13A. Contact someone outside of the district.

13B. Write down a list of why you chose the teaching profession as a career and consider discussing your second thoughts with an outside career counselor. If possible, take a day off from school and visit a working colleague in a different profession.

MONEY

14A. Contact the HR department or the business manager.

14B. Make sure that you are reading the pay stub correctly and compare it closely with your contract. If you are expected to perform extra duties, those stipends may not appear during the first few paychecks of the school year.

15A. Contact the HR department or the business manager.

15B. Check with your personal financial adviser about various tax-sheltered programs outside of the school before checking with the district's business department. Have all of your retirement options and plans available to discuss before meeting with the appropriate human resources person.

16A. Ask your mentor. Look over the school district field trip guidelines.

16B. The district should have a set of rules and regulations for setting up field trips which should include the minimum number of chaperones as well as how and when to collect money. Check to see if there is a special fund for students who cannot afford the cost of the trip. Don't forget that transportation can be very expensive; plan well ahead of the expected date.

17A. Check with the curriculum coordinator, principal, staff developer, or your mentor.

17B. Make copies of the membership application forms for the various organizations you would like to join. The district may have a schoolwide group membership. Check to see if there is a short-term trial membership option. Ask other teachers if they belong and if they enjoy member benefits of the group you would like to join.

18A. Contact the business manager, human resources, or your principal.

18B. Normally, one would need to get permission ahead of time before attending a workshop or event in order to get reimbursement. Be sure to have all documents that indicated what you paid and include other costs such as meals and transportation. You may be reimbursed for everything, especially if the district's professional development funds have not reached their target expenditure.

FELLOW STAFF MEMBERS

19A. Contact your mentor and/or human resources department.

19B. Make sure that you are being harassed as this can be a very serious charge. Record the dates and times of the situations that took place that lead you to believe that you were harassed. Review the district policy about harassment and then make an appointment with the human resources department.

20A. Set up a time to meet with your mentor.

20B. Find out first what issues the union is planning to address and decide if you want to take part. It may be a simple informational meeting. If you find yourself in the very unfortunate situation of a possible strike, you may want to consult with other beginning, nontenured teachers to get a feel for what they intend to do.

21A. Make an appointment with the special education director.

21B. Reread the student's IEP carefully to make sure that you understand what modifications need to take place. Review your own lesson plans to see if you carried out the designated modifications. Also speak with the student case manager and the teacher who is questioning your plan together and discuss the issues.

22A. Contact your mentor.

22B. Try bringing the cliques together to dig into basic curriculum goals and instructional objectives. Since that is your road map for your classroom teaching and lesson plans, that should afford you a chance to remain neutral and stay on common ground.

STUDENTS

23A. Speak with the principal or school counselor. Let them call the police, not you.

23B. Do your best to identify the student(s) in question and then turn the paper over to the proper school authorities. Don't try to do this one yourself.

24A. Contact your mentor or fellow teachers who have this same student.

24B. Work with the school counselor to see if this student has any particular family issues or problems outside of school. Investigate to see who has had this student before and see if that person may be able to offer some solutions.

25A. Contact the school district test administrator.

25B. Thank the student for his or her honesty and ask the student to identify the person he or she thought was cheating. Tell the child who informed you about the cheating that his or her response will be kept between you and the administrator. Explain that you will not let the cheater know who made the report.

CHAPTER 3

How Can We Make This Work?

MENTORS OVERCOMING OBSTACLES

How to Use This Chapter

People entering the education profession are a diverse group. Some enter directly after a university experience; others enter after years in a different career. Occasionally, new or beginning teachers come from the same background as their mentor and share similar personality traits; most times, however, new teachers are vastly different than their mentors in many ways. Because of the diversity of the new-teacher workforce, experienced teachers must be aware of the ways that they are different than the person whom they are mentoring.

Each scenario collected in this chapter presents a problem related to a new teacher. Each new teacher in these scenarios needs some type of intervention on the part of the mentor. In order for mentors to be successful in helping the new teacher, mentors must consider their own identities, their perceptions of the new teacher in question, and the culture of the school in which they work. The new teacher at the center of each scenario may be the same or vastly different from the mentor asked to role-play a solution.

Depending on your background, personality, and experiences, you will have differentiated approaches to helping the new teacher in question. In this way, these scenarios are open-ended with no clear-cut answers.

After reading each scenario, you should consider two questions. Read each scenario carefully and respond using the two-step process outlined below.

1. What is the key issue in this scenario?
2. What specific strategies will you use in order to bring resolution to the dilemma?

Mentors have varying opinions. Some mentors will choose to advocate for their mentees, bringing other people into the process; others will resolve the conflict on their own. It is possible that the resolution to the problem could involve dissolving the mentoring relationship if all other options are exhausted.

After completing each scenario, complete the reflection scale provided. The reflection scale gives mentors the opportunity to critically evaluate their decision making.

Based on the set of scenarios, how comfortable do you feel about your action plans? Using a scale of one to five, indicate how confident and comfortable you are about your plans.

Uncertain		Good		Confident
1	2	3	4	5

Reflection upon your decisions is an extremely important part of the process as it is both an end and a beginning. If uncertainty about an action plan is present, reevaluate the decisions, do some research, speak to new people, and begin the process anew.

Scenarios

For each situation, place yourself in the role of a mentor assigned to the new teacher described.

Scenario 1. Janet is a fourth-grade teacher with one full year of teaching experience in a previous district but brand-new to your school. At the conclusion of the first quarter, in an all-school faculty meeting where different procedures were discussed, she informs you that the attendance process and lunch count procedures are not the same as in her old district. She would like to have you, as her mentor, set up a meeting with the administration in order for her to inform them that she has a better way of doing everyday procedures; she feels that she can greatly improve the efficiency of her new school based on her experiences from her previous district.

What is the key issue in this scenario?
What specific strategies will you use in order to bring resolution to the dilemma?

Scenario 2. Carmen is new to your school, but she has ten years of previous experience. Although she has expressly stated that she doesn't need a mentor, you have been able to establish a professional friendship with her. You are able to give her guidance with school policies, but she is not open to feedback about her instruction or curriculum development. You have recently become aware that Carmen has some dubious grading techniques. A student whom you previously had in class explains that Carmen often does not give assignments back with feedback, but she still puts grades into the grade book. When this student asked to see his graded work to verify his total points for the semester, Carmen dismissed his question and explained that her overall professional opinion mattered more than "numbers on paper."

What is the key issue in this scenario?
What specific strategies will you use in order to bring resolution to the dilemma?

Scenario 3. Ken is going through a divorce, and the legal proceedings are beginning to interfere with his teaching assignment. Beyond the time out of class, he has begun to exhibit signs of irritability, and the teachers around him suspect that he has not been able to keep up with his grading and planning.

What is the key issue in this scenario?
What specific strategies will you use in order to bring resolution to the dilemma?

Scenario 4. Cheryl is a 22-year-old high school teacher in her first year of teaching. It is apparent to you that she has trouble maintaining professional distance from her senior students. She has given her cell phone number to students, opened her MySpace page to her classes, and will often meet students outside of school at local coffeehouses and bookstores. Recently, she has been complaining to you about discipline issues in her classes.

What is the key issue in this scenario?
What specific strategies will you use in order to bring resolution to the dilemma?

REFLECT

Based on scenarios 1–4, how comfortable do you feel about your action plans? Using a scale of one to five, indicate how confident and comfortable you are about your plans.

Uncertain		Good		Confident
1	2	3	4	5

COMMENTS/NOTES:

Tips

HOW TO DETECT AND DISSOLVE MISMATCHES WITHOUT ANIMOSITY

- Mentors and new teachers should know that not every relationship will work out perfectly. Barry Sweeny (2003) explains that when a mentor is asked to be a part of the program, that teacher must understand that "mentor-protégé matching is an inexact science."

  It is not always possible for every mentoring partnership to produce strong bonds between mentor and new teacher; therefore, mentors must not strive for perfection but instead expect bumps in the road. Both mentors and new teachers should also be aware that they have the opportunity to request a new match if their current match is ineffective.

- Time for communication and collaboration must be a significant part of the mentoring partnership. Ed.gov (2004), in its "New Teacher Survival Guide," explains that "well-administered mentor programs that foster regular meetings between new teachers and their senior colleagues are lifesavers for first-year teachers."

  Programs that provide and promote structured time for new teachers and mentors to meet will be stronger and more productive with less chance of the relationship fading due to time apart.

- The onus of success should be on the program, not the individuals involved. It is important for new teachers and mentors to go into the relationship knowing that blame will never be placed on them if a mentor pairing is not successful.

  Likewise, it is important for mentors to remember that successful matches are the result of the combination of hard work on the part of both the new teacher and mentor, and the structures in place within the mentoring program. Celebrating success is important, but mentors must remain humble.

  The Keewatin-Patricia District School Board (2004) in Dryden, Ontario, sees the dangers of mentoring programs linked to mentors' "feelings of responsibility for success or failure, fear of being classified a know-it-all, fear of not knowing all of the answers," and competitiveness.

  It is important for all mentors to understand that strong mentoring programs encourage success for *all* new teachers; this goal cannot be achieved in an environment of fear or competition.
- Similarity of personalities is important when considering a mentor match, but similar content knowledge is a vital key to success. California's teacher support program administrator, Teri Clark, reflects that "team[ing] an art teacher with a math teacher . . . [is] a major problem" (Thissen, 2008).

  In schools that are struggling to find mentors, it is common for any two teachers to be paired regardless of teaching assignment. This causes a problem because the mentor cannot provide specific content support for planning, instruction, and assessment.

  Though these mixed subject area pairings can work, mentoring programs should strive to pair teachers who teach the same subject so that mentors can best assist new teachers.
- Program leaders should check in with mentoring pairs on a regular basis. It is important for mentors and new teachers to understand that a person in leadership cares about the partnership and is there to provide assistance whenever necessary. Sweeny (2003) finds an

additional virtue in strong leadership as he urges leaders "to emphasize that there will be a mismatch check with *every* mentoring pair.

"This is vital so that if it becomes necessary to discuss a mismatch, the people will not feel 'singled out.'" In this way, any potential issues can be detected early and resolution found before they
result in a dissolved partnership.

Scenario 5. Janine, a single mother of two, must pick up her children
at day care by 3:30 p.m.; however, the new contract negotiated by
the union stipulates that the official workday ends at 3:45 p.m. She
could change day-care centers to a place with a later pickup time, but
it would cost her money that she does not have.

What is the key issue in this scenario?
What specific strategies will you use in order to bring resolution to
the dilemma?

Scenario 6. Bill, a new teacher you have been working with since
the beginning of the year, has just received his termination papers.
Although you knew he was struggling a bit, you had no idea that
he was going to be let go. You feel that, as his assigned mentor, you
could have provided more intervention strategies but you were left
"out in the cold" and not informed of the administration's intentions
to deliver a pink slip. You feel let down, if not betrayed, by the administration, and you are now considering not serving as a mentor in
future years.

What is the key issue in this scenario?
What specific strategies will you use in order to bring resolution to
the dilemma?

Scenario 7. Angelo is doing a very good job as a first-year teacher.
As a mentee, he has been easy to work with; he is proactive, open to

feedback, and genuinely concerned with the success of his students. Lately, he has begun to complain that he feels underappreciated. In addition to that, he is constantly worried about his job security for the next school year; no one has told him he is doing well. It is clear that Angelo needs consistent praise in order to feel good about his performance as a new teacher.

What is the key issue in this scenario?
What specific strategies will you use in order to bring resolution to the dilemma?

Scenario 8. James, an army reservist, must miss school one Monday a month because of his commitment, and he may need to miss up to a week of school just after spring break. Although he explained this commitment in the interview process, he fears that he will not find consistency with his classes with the amount of time he is out of the classroom.

What is the key issue in this scenario?
What specific strategies will you use in order to bring resolution to the dilemma?

REFLECT

Based on scenarios 5–8, how comfortable do you feel about your action plans? Using a scale of one to five, indicate how confident and comfortable you are about your plans.

Uncertain		Good		Confident
1	2	3	4	5

COMMENTS/NOTES:

Tips

CAREER CHANGERS AS PROTÉGÉS

- Most new teachers aren't entering the profession without some type of previous professional experience. Paula Rutherford (2005) states, "According to a January 2000 Issue Brief published by the National Governors' Association (NGA) Center for Best Practices, that year 55 percent of the candidates entering teacher preparation programs at the graduate level and 11 percent at the undergraduate level entered teaching from career fields other than education."

  Mentors must understand that adults are entering the education profession with previous experiences that are diverse and strongly influential on their teaching styles. Consider how mentoring a former vice president of marketing may differ from mentoring a new teacher fresh out of the university.

- Teachers who have changed careers are adult learners, and they have needs. Rutherford (2005) asserts that because career changers are adult learners, they "need to be validated for what they already know and do . . . we need to recognize and build on their experience."

  Career changers have valid experiences that they bring to the table. Lawyers, doctors, military service people, businesspeople, and tradespeople will be able to contribute unique points of view to their classrooms.

Mentors should never diminish the accomplishments from a former career of the new teacher; rather, the mentor should seek to help new teachers incorporate this vast base of knowledge into practice.

- They are in it for the right reasons. C. E. Feistritzer in *Profile of Alternate Route Teachers* explains that "those entering the teaching profession through an alternate route cite a desire to work with young people and contribute something of value to society as their primary reasons for wanting to become teachers" (ASCD, 2006).

Career changers have put much thought and effort into their new career paths. A mentor should respect the desire of these new teachers to bring about change in education. Career changers are often "placed where demand is greatest—urban and rural areas—and teach high-demand subjects such as special education, mathematics, and science" (Feistritzer in ASCD, 2006).

Mentors should understand and embrace career changers as adults who have chosen education as a career because they have genuine interest in teaching, *not* because they were unsuccessful in their previous career.

- But . . . career changers need strong, on-the-job training and a dedicated mentor. Mary Lord (2000) attributes "emergency [teacher] licensing programs" to "swelling school-age populations and efforts to reduce class size."

Many career changers may earn a teaching certificate in a greatly truncated program. "These quickie courses can run from a few days to a few weeks . . . but Stanford's [Linda] Darling-Hammond, who has done comparative studies, says crash courses often lack academic rigor and fail to provide students with sufficient mentoring" (Lord, 2000). Though career changers have the desire to teach, they lack the extensive practical experience of the mentor.

- Career changers need the most help in the area of classroom management. Career changers often enter teaching with strong organizational skills. Most career changers understand how to navigate interpersonal relationships and pick up on the culture of schools.

But as former civil engineer Mark Martin explains, "We didn't get enough about dealing with kids [in teacher preparation courses]" (Kopkowski, 2006).

Telecommunications manager Jada Overton reinforces this idea as she says, "'You learn about the mechanics of how a school runs, but [not enough] about how to actually teach the kids.' It was through observing her mentor and each day's experiences in the classroom that she honed those skills" (Kopkowski, 2006).

Just like new teachers right out of the university, career changers need the practical experience of working with children and adolescents in order to improve their classroom skills. Just because many career changers have managed adults in previous careers, strong modeling by a mentor can make all the difference in the tricky art of classroom management of young people.

Scenario 9. Linda is a first-year teacher who had taken time off from the accounting world to raise her children. Rather than return to accounting she pursued a career in education. She taught sixth grade and followed scripted lesson plans and the book. She is a very static teacher who built relationships well with students. Parents had made numerous phone calls regarding the amount of homework assigned. During the school's open house she gave a five-minute presentation showing a narrow view of the sixth-grade curriculum and limited student work.

What is the key issue in this scenario?
What specific strategies will you use in order to bring resolution to the dilemma?

Scenario 10. Miguel, a math teacher, must use crutches to walk because of a genetic disease that affected his spine in childhood. This has never impeded him in his teaching assignment, but the building where he works does not have an elevator. His classroom and office are on the second level of the building with the rest of the math department, and although he can use the stairs, it creates an unnecessary burden for him. He requested a classroom and an office on the first floor, but he has not yet been accommodated.

What is the key issue in this scenario?
What specific strategies will you use in order to bring resolution to the dilemma?

Scenario 11. At an end-of-the-year wrap-up session run by an outside consultant, all of the mentors and new teachers in your school are meeting. Sitting on one side of the room and discussing their roles is a group of mentors while the new teachers are involved in an evaluation discussion on the other side. One of the new teachers informs the discussion leader that her first year of teaching went so smoothly that she needed to create imaginary classroom problems in order to make her mentor feel good about helping her with her new teaching position. At the end of the workshop session, the discussion leader relates this troubling story to all of the mentors.

What is the key issue in this scenario?
What specific strategies will you use in order to bring resolution to the dilemma?

Scenario 12. As a conservative Jewish man, Ben will miss days of school in order to attend synagogue and family functions. He is worried that he will be ostracized because he is taking many days off as a new teacher, and perhaps because of his devout religious beliefs.

What is the key issue in this scenario?
What specific strategies will you use in order to bring resolution to the dilemma?

REFLECT

Based on scenarios 9–12, how comfortable do you feel about your action plans? Using a scale of one to five, indicate how confident and comfortable you are about your plans.

Uncertain		Good		Confident
1	2	3	4	5

COMMENTS/NOTES:

Tips

TAKING GENERATIONAL DIFFERENCES INTO ACCOUNT

- Difference in age between mentor and protégé should be regarded seriously. Oftentimes, there is a gap in age between mentors and their protégés. The most traditional pairing is an older, more experienced teacher with a younger, inexperienced teacher right out of the university.

  Consider a nontraditional pairing like a thirty-something experienced teacher paired with a fifty-something protégé who has just changed careers. Are there issues that can crop up with a younger person mentoring a new teacher who is older?

  Although age can be a neutral variable in mentoring partnerships, understanding generational differences can make for more compatible mentoring matches. This isn't to say that each individual teacher doesn't have his or her unique personality, but age can be a strong factor in determining good matches.

• Generational differences run deeper than simply a gap in age between mentor and new teacher. Paula Rutherford (2005) explains that "values and actions are also shaped by personal and world events that occurred at a given point in our lives." In general, generational differences can account for differences in personality and workplace interactions. Baby boomers are "loyal to employers, enjoy working in teams, and will practice . . . for far longer than really necessary. [Millenials are] fluent with technology and full of positive energy" (Flannery, 2008).

Mentoring pairs of different generations can truly complement one another, but mentors must be aware of how a person of a different generation, whether older or younger, approaches the job. This understanding can be the difference between a harmonious relationship and one fraught with misunderstandings.

When considering mentoring pairs, here are some general characteristics of people from different generations, adapted from Rutherford (2005) and Flannery (2008).

Baby Boomers: Born 1942–1960

Values:	Personality characteristics:	Workplace style:
• Competition • Hard work • Success • Equality	• Assertive • Loyal • Dedicated • Inclusive • Optimistic	• May work too hard at tasks • Better at linear tasks that include concrete processes • Enjoy teamwork • Always willing to put in the time to go the extra mile

Generation X'ers: Born 1960–1980

Values:	Personality characteristics:	Workplace style:
• Diversity • Balance • Relationships • Trust • Patience	• Self-reliant • Independent • Creative • Energetic	• Informal • Action: Rutherford (2005) says they like to "*do* rather than listen and watch." • Enjoy special assignments • Abstract thinkers who may curtail the set process and create their own

Millenials: Born 1980–2005

Values:	Personality characteristics:	Workplace style:
• Family • Technology • Autonomy • Diversity	• Flexible • Enthusiastic • Optimistic • Patient	• Multitasking • Use humor and fun • Use technology in creative, time-saving ways • Graciously accept (and expect) praise for a job well done

Scenario 13. Betty is a high-achieving perfectionist and is a teacher's aide for Mr. James's fourth-grade class. Being an ambitious over-achiever, she began taking courses toward her teacher certification. Mr. James was promoted to building principal and then hired Betty as his fourth-grade teacher. The principal regularly features creative and enriching activities in Betty's classroom in his periodic staff newsletters while neglecting all other staff members.

What is the key issue in this scenario?
What specific strategies will you use in order to bring resolution to the dilemma?

Scenario 14. Rajit has been experiencing some difficulty in his department because a teacher has taken to teasing him about his accent. Although he and this teacher started out as collaborative and friendly colleagues, Rajit feels that the teasing crosses the line, and other department members, though they don't tease, laugh at the colleague's jokes. He has approached the colleague but has not had success resolving the problem.

What is the key issue in this scenario?
What specific strategies will you use in order to bring resolution to the dilemma?

Scenario 15. Loretta is forty-five years old. She and her partner have been married for fifteen years. She wants to display pictures of their life together on her desk, but she does not know how tolerant her co-workers will be. She has been open with many of them that she is in a committed relationship with another woman, but she is still unsure how this will affect the office environment.

What is the key issue in this scenario?
What specific strategies will you use in order to bring resolution to the dilemma?

Scenario 16. Vernon teaches math to sixth and seventh graders. He shows potential to be an excellent educator; he is meticulously organized; enthusiastic; and, in his own right, he is a superb mathematician. It is clear, however, to one of his colleagues, that he may have a learning disability associated with his writing. The language arts teacher on his team noticed that homework sheets Vernon constructed have multiple misspellings and grammatical mistakes that should have easily been noticed and corrected. Upon bringing this up with Vernon, he dismisses them because his area of teaching is math and not language arts.

What is the key issue in this scenario?
What specific strategies will you use in order to bring resolution to the dilemma?

REFLECT

Based on scenarios 13–16, how comfortable do you feel about your action plans? Using a scale of one to five, indicate how confident and comfortable you are about your plans.

Uncertain		Good		Confident
1	2	3	4	5

COMMENTS/NOTES:

Tips

ADDITIONAL ROLES OF THE MENTOR

Mentors are often chosen because they have superior knowledge when it comes to teaching students effectively. It is hard to present an experienced mentor with a situation he or she cannot handle. Often masters of classroom management, mentors can deftly dole out advice on how to resolve the toughest of classroom situations.

But mentors need to provide more coaching to new teachers that goes beyond the daily challenges that arise in the classroom. Here are a few of the many additional roles that effective mentors must take on.

- Mentors need to be encouragers. Reiman (1999) points out that every new teacher has times of success as well as periods of doubt. New teachers need praise when they have success and encouragement when times are tough. Mentors act as guides and role models, but they must also be highly concerned with the motivational and affective needs of new teachers.

  In the first years, it can be the emotional struggles that pin down new teachers. A mentor who understands these needs of a new teacher can be a strong ally.
- Excellent communication is an invaluable skill for mentors. Communication is a multipronged skill. Mentors must be able to listen carefully, respond empathetically, and give guidance clearly.

  Rutherford (2005) suggests "keep[ing] an open-door policy complemented with daily communication." This way, new teachers know that mentors are approachable, but mentors also have a way to open avenues of communication if a mentee is hesitant to ask for guidance. It goes without saying that great mentors strive to form deep, meaningful relationships with new teachers, and positive, clear communication goes a long way.
- Mentors must be advocates. Because new teachers have little experience, they may need a mentor to take an active role in guiding them toward a positive workplace experience. Burke (2002) says that an expectation of the mentor is to "arrange for introductions to other staff members, administrators, and school personnel."

  For some protégés, a new teaching job may be their first career, and they need coaching beyond teaching students; they need help navigating a professional work environment.

  Although we all try to have friendly, supportive workplaces, the reality is that there may be times when a new teacher is taken advantage of. A mentor should not hesitate to be a positive voice for a new teacher. The mentor should not *always* have to step in; mentors should also promote polite assertiveness on the part of the protégé if further confronted with these circumstances.

• Mentors should be models of the cultures and structures of their school. New teachers have enough to worry about in the classroom, but it can be what happens in the office that makes or breaks them. Mentors should be keenly aware that a protégé also needs to learn how to interact positively with other school employees.

Interestingly, one of the most important facets of the workplace for new teachers is school climate and leadership. A Duke study asserts "that principal leadership and school climate deserve more attention . . . [than] salary hikes" in the retention of new teachers (Gilmer, 2006). New teachers need modeling in how to interact with administrators and coworkers; they must be able to recognize the nuances of the professional environment specific to their school.

Mentors not only have more experience teaching students, they have more experience in the school in which they teach. Sharing these experiences with protégés is an essential facet of mentoring.

Scenario 17. Dante, a fifth-grade teacher, is one of the most gifted new teachers you have ever worked with. He is a true professional in every sense of the word. His teaching methods are strong, his students genuinely like him, and he is a fantastic youth basketball coach. One issue that continues to be brought up by colleagues is Dante's personal hygiene and style of dress. His hair is often uncombed, and he doesn't shave regularly. His clothes are mismatched, wrinkled, and often have stains or holes.

What is the key issue in this scenario?
What specific strategies will you use in order to bring resolution to the dilemma?

Scenario 18. Victoria's previous experience as an educator has been in a juvenile detention center. Although she has learned excellent classroom management skills, some of her methods are extremely stringent. She is clearly a gifted teacher, but her students do not often require strict interventions. Victoria's students have begun to complain to other teachers that they are being treated unfairly; colleagues have begun to describe her techniques as old-fashioned and bordering on cruelty.

What is the key issue in this scenario?
What specific strategies will you use in order to bring resolution to the dilemma?

Scenario 19. George is a first-year high school chemistry teacher. George graduated from his university with the state chemical engineering award. He has developed strong relationships with students and he has proven himself successful with parents. Just before the winter holiday break, he was cited for a messy chemical storage room and obtained quotes from a chemical removal company. The principal felt that by going over his head, George had overstepped his bounds.

What is the key issue in this scenario?
What specific strategies will you use in order to bring resolution to the dilemma?

Scenario 20. Lydia has Crohn's disease and sometimes suffers from intense stomach cramps. Her symptoms can be unexpected and so severe that she must leave class without warning. She is worried about classroom management and the possible embarrassment she would face from students and other teachers if she has to leave the room without notice.

What is the key issue in this scenario?
What specific strategies will you use in order to bring resolution to the dilemma?

REFLECT

Based on scenarios 17–20, how comfortable do you feel about your action plans? Using a scale of one to five, indicate how confident and comfortable you are about your plans.

Uncertain		Good		Confident
1	2	3	4	5

COMMENTS/NOTES:

References

Association for Supervision and Curriculum Development (ASCD). (2006, March). Teaching, the second time around. *Education Update* 48(3), 1–8.

Burke, Kay. (2002). *Mentoring guidebook: Mapping the journey.* Arlington Heights, IL: SkyLight Professional Development.

DePaul, Amy. (2004, September 14). *Survival guide for new teachers: Working with principles.* Retrieved July 30, 2008, from http://www.ed.gov/teachers/become/about/survivalguide/principal.html.

Flannery, Mary Ellen. (2008, February). Playing the generation game. *NEA Today*, 40–41.

Gilmer, Kelly. (2006, April 12). Principal leadership, school climate critical to retaining beginning teachers, Duke study finds. Retrieved July 18, 2008, from http://news.duke.edu/2006/04/retention.html.

Keewatin-Patricia District School Board. (2004, July). *Mentorship program.* Retrieved July 30, 2008, from http://www.kpdsb.on.ca/education/edu-Mentorship.asp.

Kopkowski, Cynthia. (2006, March). Swapping the boardroom for the classroom. *NEA Today*, 32–33.

Lord, Mary. (2000, April 10). The ranks of teachers are swelling with former pilots, lobbyists, and lawyers. *U.S. News and World Report*, 91–92.

Reiman, A. J. (1999, August). The evolution of the social roletaking and guided reflection framework in teacher education: Recent theory and quantitative synthesis of research. *Teaching and Teacher Education*, 15(6), 597–612.

Rutherford, Paula. (2005). *21st Century mentor's handbook: Creating a culture for learning.* Alexandria, VA: Just ASK Publications.

Sweeny, Barry. (2003). *Dealing with a mentor-protege mismatch.* Retrieved July 30, 2008, from http://www.mentoring-association.org/MembersOnly/Process/Mismatch.html.

Thissen, Paul. (2008, January 4). *Teacher-mentor program falls short, critics contend.* Retrieved July 30, 2008, from http://findarticles.com/p/articles/mi_qn4176/is_20080104/ ai_n21189764.

CHAPTER 4

Isn't My Mentor Supposed to Help Me?

WHEN MENTORS AND NEW TEACHERS STRUGGLE TO CONNECT WITH EACH OTHER

How to Use This Chapter

Mentors are experienced teachers who have the important task of giving assistance to new teachers. Acting as role model, guide, and advocate, the mentor ensures the comfort and growth of a teacher in a new position. Sometimes, new teachers have exceptional success in the classroom during their first year. This presents a new challenge for mentors; they must provide support while also supporting the independent success of new teachers.

We have recorded ten case studies that present dilemmas that affect mentoring relationships, and it is up to both the mentor and the new teacher to analyze the stories in order to understand how the relationship between mentor and mentee could be improved.

You are called upon to recognize the successes and failures of the mentors in each case study. New teachers should recognize how the behaviors of their counterparts in each story make it easy or difficult for the experienced teachers to mentor. Whether you are a mentor or a new teacher, each case study asks you to identify the issues and then explore ways to resolve the problem based on a series of questions for further thought.

Each case study presents a unique challenge, and they all require teachers to differentiate their style based on the desired outcome. How you approach each situation will be dictated by your personality, teaching style, perceptions, and the culture of the school in which you work. In this way, these case studies create a differentiated activity that provides an experience tailored to your needs.

Age Gaps

Claudia received a bachelor of fine arts degree in 1986 with an area of concentration in keyboard music performance. Although she wanted to work in the public schools as a general music teacher, she decided to remain at home and raise three children. Her husband, who worked for a successful business firm, was about to lose his job. Knowing that her husband could soon be out of work, Claudia decided to go back to school and get her classroom teaching certificate and begin a new career in education at the age of forty-four.

"Although I volunteered for many years in my children's class-rooms as a room mother and helper for students who had difficulties with reading, I knew that I always wanted to be a classroom teacher myself. I felt I could contribute my talents and help children learn to love reading and math."

Claudia completed a master's degree program and did her student teaching in a fifth-grade classroom. After several interviews, she secured a teaching position in a sixth-grade classroom in an elementary school just outside of Philadelphia.

"The school was terrific and very welcoming. I was excited to work with my assigned mentor, Mary, to help me through the many challenges that come with the territory. We met several times to review the curriculum and learning goals before the students arrived. We established a solid relationship and were off to a great start, though it was never made clear to me what Mary's role and obligations were going to be as the year progressed."

The school year started and just about caught Claudia off guard. She had several special needs students in her class; three children did not speak English; parents questioned her reading instruction methods. Even though her mentor was just across the hallway, Claudia often hesitated to ask questions for help.

"I felt overwhelmed with the demands of meeting the needs of so many students of diverse backgrounds. Schools had certainly changed. Testing, meeting standards, differentiation, formative and summative assessments were all new to me. During class, I kept a small notebook and would write down questions that would pop up during the day that I would ask my mentor, or at this point, whoever would listen and help out.

"My mentor, who was actually ten years my younger, started to show signs of getting tired of me. When I went to her for help, I thought I was walking on eggshells. I knew I had some other allies in school, but I found myself so loaded with questions that I became consumed with trying to decide who to go to for help."

October was fast approaching; that meant parent/teacher conferences, report cards, special education staff meetings, and the expectation to attend a variety of evening programs. Claudia soon switched into survival mode. She felt that since she was an older teacher in the school that she should feel far more comfortable with teaching than she was.

She had terrific reviews from her principal but was starting to feel pressure from her mentor that she should be doing a better job. Ironically, the only advice she was now getting from Mary was, "Just relax and take a deep breath. Tomorrow will be better."

"Well, truth be told, I did take deep breaths and started to make priorities and not feel I needed to accomplish everything at once. I was also at a turning point with my mentor. Although she was a nice person, I really felt our relationship was not going to develop any further and that I was on my own.

"With Thanksgiving around the corner, I decided to be thankful for the teaching position I had and to just carry out on my own. The assigning of a mentor was a nice idea, but it didn't amount to anything when I really needed a mentor's help. I just hope I can make it to the end of the year on my own."

QUESTIONS FOR FURTHER THOUGHT

1. All indications show that Claudia was an outstanding first-year teacher, but her mentor was giving her the cold shoulder. How should Claudia have handled the situation knowing that the school year was not even half over, and it was apparent that her mentor was giving up on her?
2. Would it have been more helpful for both Claudia and her mentor to have clearly defined roles and a better understanding of the expectations of the school district's new-teacher induction program?
3. What are some critical issues that could develop when the mentor is ten years younger than the new teacher?
4. Do you think that the cold shoulder effect Claudia was feeling from her mentor was is part due to the fact that Claudia was seeking help and advice from many other sources? Could it be that the mentor decided to "give up" on their relationship because Claudia went elsewhere for advice?

ANOTHER LOOK

Boreen et al. (2009) make a very clear assertion regarding age difference between mentors and mentees:

> An age difference of eight to fifteen years is recommended so that the mentor is viewed as experienced. The age difference may be important even for nontraditional beginning teachers . . . The disparity should not be so wide, however, that a parenting relationship develops. Sometimes, too, age

differences can be generational differences. When ages vary considerably, the mentor pair need [*sic*] to appreciate their differences rather than seek similarities.

The following factors should be considered in forming a mentoring partnership. If possible, a mentor should:

- Have a minimum of three to five years of teaching experience
- Be teaching in the same content area or at the same grade level as the beginning teacher
- Have a classroom close to that of the beginning teacher
- Be significantly older than the beginning teacher

Interestingly, Boreen et al. (2009) stipulate that age, an uncontrollable condition, must be seriously considered when assigning mentor pairs. In many schools there may not be an opportunity to pair a willing mentor and a new teacher with enough of an age difference to accommodate Boreen's guidelines.

Now, more than ever, people are entering the teaching profession at a later age. If a teacher begins her career at the age of forty-six, that would require a willing mentor who is 54–61 years old. Even if a teacher falls into this age range, what guarantee is there that the grade level, subject area, or classroom location of this teacher is comparable to the new teacher's?

Indeed, the inflexibility of having to be "substantially older" than a mentee may divert the willingness of younger teachers to become mentors. In many schools, being an older teacher is often equated with having many years of experience, but the age of new teachers entering the profession continues to rise, thus providing challenges to mentoring programs that rely on an age gap as a predictor of success in mentoring pairs.

Many businesses have turned to a "reverse-mentoring" model in order to bridge the gap between older employees and their younger colleagues. In this model, it is the younger colleague who instructs the older in new techniques and technology. Consider this anecdote from Kapos (2007):

> Carlos Martinez, 47, is an architect and regional design director at Gensler with 23 years of experience. Six years ago, when he joined the firm—where the median age is about 30—he teamed up with Kate Clemens Davis, now 32 and a senior associate and interior designer.
>
> As he acclimated to the younger workplace, he says, he appreciated her ability to deal with issues in a more off-the-cuff way, a tactic he now uses to his advantage.
>
> While his generation might approach a problem with a full-blown meeting—steno pad and pen in hand—"she'll parachute to my desk and ask a simple question and we'll have a short discussion on a topic. It's very impromptu. I do the same thing now."

In this case, a younger person was able to mentor an older person with success. The age gap, in this case, was not an issue.

Regardless of age, the bottom line is that mentors must have significant teaching experience. A thirty-year-old may have up to nine years experience of teaching. This individual has a wealth of knowledge to share with a new teacher, even if that new teacher happens to be much older.

Although they may be stringent about an age gap, Boreen et al. (2009) do make one concession: "while age is significant, the maturity levels of the participants are even more important." Indeed, an experienced, willing, mature mentor is an experienced, willing, mature mentor regardless of age.

Recognizing Boundaries

Lilly is a 23-year-old new teacher. She has gotten her dream job in a suburban elementary school in the grade of her choice, second grade.

She has established an incredibly strong collegial relationship with her mentor, Karen.

As Lilly explains, "Karen has given me the benefit of her twenty-five years of teaching. Any time that I have a question or concern, Karen is there to help. She has truly been the one person that I can count on all of the time." Lilly has expressed that Karen is a "master teacher," one brilliantly capable of teaching children subject matter and learning-for-life abilities. Lilly mentions that she "looks up to Karen" and that "she hopes to be the kind of teacher that Karen is" as she continues her own career.

Lilly is a superb new teacher. She takes risks in the classroom in order to give her students novel, meaningful experiences. She is highly reflective and thoughtful about her practice; she has already established highly effective methods with which new teachers often struggle in their first years. Simply stated, Lilly is a superb new teacher.

Although Lilly thinks very highly of Karen's teaching and her mentoring ability, it became apparent to Lilly in the second half of the year that she wanted to establish more independence. Gradually, Lilly and Karen tapered off the amount of time that they would meet on a weekly basis in order to accommodate Lilly's wishes of independence.

Lilly relates that "Karen has been amazingly willing to give me my space. She understands how to pull back and let me go on my own." In fact, Karen and Lilly have established a partnering model that works well for both of them.

Lilly explains, "I feel more like a professional colleague with Karen than I do a mentee. What I mean is that Karen asks me for advice, and I ask her for the same. We bounce ideas off of one another instead of me just asking her for advice. It's been really nice being able to find a place where my opinion matters. I'm not just the new teacher. I am also a contributor to the 2nd grade team."

Lilly is extremely happy with the professional relationship that she has been able to establish with Karen and the other second-grade teachers, but a problem has begun to present itself. The other teachers, especially Karen, have begun to ask Lilly to make social plans outside of school. Karen is married and has three children. Often, the social plans include Karen's husband and children as well as the spouses and children of other teachers.

Lilly feels awkward around the families of other teachers. "I love Karen and the other teachers, but spending time with their families is hard for me. I am in my early twenties, and Karen is in her late forties. She has children that are teenagers. I don't have anything in common with her in terms of our social lives. They like to go bowling and have barbecues. My friends and I go to clubs. When I was invited to a Christmas party at Karen's house, I felt like the oldest child that desperately wants to be somewhere else besides with the older crowd."

As Karen and Lilly have gotten closer professionally, Karen continues to ask Lilly to spend time with her family. Lilly has begun to make excuses about why she cannot spend time with Karen outside of school; many times these excuses are fake.

"I feel terrible for making up reasons that I can't see Karen, but I feel that I would make it worse if I told her straight out that I don't want to see her socially outside of school. I have asked Karen out for dinner, just the two of us, but she just turns it around on me and asks me over to her house for dinner with the family. Karen has been the best mentor. I don't want to hurt her feelings by always turning her down."

As the school year comes to a close, Lilly has expressed that her relationship with Karen has become awkward. After a number of times when Lilly rebuffed Karen's invitations, it was clear to Lilly that "Karen started to act differently towards me at school. We used to talk all the time about her family, but now Karen rarely mentions anything about her time outside of school. It also feels like it has carried over into my relationships with some of the other second-grade teachers.

"Where we once used to openly talk about our social lives, I feel isolated from these kinds of conversations. I feel out of the loop. Karen didn't even tell me that her son got into college. That would have been something she would have told me first thing in the morning over coffee."

Lilly feels that because she did not accept Karen's social calls, her professional relationship has been damaged. "Maybe I should have gone over to Karen's home a couple of times to show her that I value her friendship. I want to be friends with Karen, but our age gap is an issue for me.

"I can't ask Karen out with my younger friends, and I don't want to be the odd person out at her family get-togethers." Furthermore, Lilly feels like she "lost a great mentor. I don't feel like my teaching is as good without the closeness I had with Karen."

QUESTIONS FOR FURTHER THOUGHT

1. What are Lilly's responsibilities as the new teacher to resolve this dilemma? What are Karen's responsibilities as the mentor?
2. Did Karen overstep a boundary as a mentoring teacher in asking Lilly for social plans?
3. Could Lilly have avoided this situation? Would there have been a way for her to continue her strong collegial bond while also declining Karen's social calls?
4. What have Lilly and Karen done well in their mentoring relationship? What were their missteps?

ANOTHER LOOK

The bond that Lilly and Karen formed is common in mentoring relationships, especially when much thought goes into the pairing. Becoming friends immediately, however, is not necessarily the best thing for a mentoring partnership.

Finkelstein and Poteet (2007) explain that "mentors have an obligation to maintain appropriate boundaries since they have the most power in the relationship. In addition to valuing respect and avoiding misuse of power, mentors should initiate regular conversation about the nature of the mentoring relationship. What needs of mine (as a mentor) are being met in this relationship that would be better met in a different relationship that did not have a power differential?"

Karen may have overstepped boundaries that she should have set for her mentoring relationship with Lilly. There is nothing wrong with being friendly and caring, but inviting Lilly over to her home crossed a line.

The University of Minnesota's Counseling and Consulting Services (2008) agrees with Finkelstein and Poteet's analysis; "despite claims to the contrary, mentees are often unaware of the negative consequences associated with voluntary boundary violations; therefore, responsibility for maintaining boundaries generally resides with the mentor." Karen's actions were surely not intentional and may be a result of poor mentor training. Regardless, mentors can learn from her mistakes.

Consider these points by Lisa Bottomley (2007):

Poor boundaries in a mentoring relationship can result in:

- The mentor or mentee feeling that he or she cannot say no to—or disagree with—one another
- Anxiety and discomfort on both sides
- A mentor or mentee having codependent and unclear expectations
- A mentee who feels like a victim
- The development of one-sided relationships—with no give-and-take
- Feelings of over-responsibility

It is obvious that Karen and Lilly enjoy each other's company and would have been friends even if their mentoring partnership had not brought them together. The lesson here is that mentors and mentees must first dissolve their formal partnership before crossing boundaries that could jeopardize their professional relationship.

Career Changers

After working for twenty-one years as a design consultant for a major architectural firm in Manhattan, Ben decided that he was ready for a major career change. He read about a fast-track teaching certification program for people with a bachelor's degree where he could earn an M.A. degree in education, along with a teaching certificate, in less than one year.

Acceptance in the program was contingent upon a rigorous academic-based entrance test, plus at least fifteen years of success in the business community. The program included an abbreviated student teaching component compared to the typical experience of an undergraduate student.

"It all seemed like a dream come true. I always wanted to be a high school math teacher, and this seemed like the ticket. The courses were offered at a time and location near my home and architectural firm. I could continue to work at my profession and earn the degree at the same time.

"The student teaching was completed during a six-week summer school program at a local school. Even before I completed the program, I had numerous interviews at several area high schools and ended up with three offers. Needless to say, things were moving at a breakneck pace."

Ben met his mentor, a fellow math teacher, during the new-teacher orientation program. His mentor, Vanessa, had twelve years of experience teaching high school math at five different schools across the country. She was excited to explore the possibility of co-teaching some classes during the year, especially knowing that Ben's rich background in architecture could be a real-world example to students of how math was used in a career.

Ben reflected, "I was looking forward to bringing my career background as personal testimony to the students in my classes about the need to study math. I checked out the district's curriculum and state goals for learning and felt there was, in fact, room to accomplish the objectives and bring in my rich background of experiences, including inviting some of my fellow colleagues to be guest speakers."

Even though Ben's experience working with high school students and teaching in general was rather short, his first semester took off with very few glitches. The students took a liking to him, and the typical first-year teacher issues such as discipline, classroom management, and keeping up with the seemingly endless piles of paperwork did not bog down his day-to-day lessons.

He enjoyed going to school every day, and he was almost beginning to wonder, "What's the big deal about being a first-year teacher?"

His ease with teaching did not go unnoticed by other staff members and especially his mentor, Vanessa.

"Although my relationship with my mentor was great, I actually felt very little need to sit down and discuss many of the typical first-year concerns that new teachers often experience. In fact, I found our intended roles reversing as she began asking me if I had any teaching tips on how to spice up her math lessons.

"I, of course, obliged, and I gave her numerous teaching ideas that I had picked up by searching the Internet for cool ideas as well as from my past experiences at the architecture firm. When I had guest speakers, we combined classes as often as possible. To my surprise, several of her students asked me if they could transfer from her classroom into one of my class sections."

In early December, Ben was surprised to find a letter in his mailbox stating that he was nominated for the city's "Best First Year Teacher" award. The letter asked him to complete a form as part of the application process. One portion was a few questions to be completed by a colleague who best knew his teaching methods and successful strategies.

His first thought was to ask Vanessa, but he thought that would be quite awkward. After all, he was supposed to be the "new kid on the block" and not the go-to person. Since the application was not due until after spring break, he had some time to think it over before deciding whom to go to in order to complete the application.

QUESTIONS FOR FURTHER THOUGHT

1. Should Ben have asked Vanessa to complete his teacher award nomination form? Or would it have been better to ask another colleague?

2. Would it have been better for the two to have a frank discussion about how their relationship should progress given the fact that the mentor/mentee roles were clearly reversed?

3. How should Ben handle the fact that students in Vanessa's room want to switch to his?

4. What are the pros and cons of various fast-track and/or alternative certification programs? Do they have pretty good track records?

ANOTHER LOOK

Consider Vanessa's approach to helping Ben transition into a career in education; she knew that it was important for him to bring his previous experiences as an architect into the classroom.

Although it seems like Vanessa was not able to provide all of the mentoring that Ben needed, she approached her relationship with him as an opportunity to expose students to a person successful in a field that greatly relies on mathematics. She respected the unique perspectives that Ben would bring from his previous career, and she recognized his teaching talent immediately.

Ben's success may seem atypical to experienced mentors. But consider that many career changers have already reached high levels of achievement in their previous careers. In order to have been successful in other professions, they already possessed personality qualities that would make them fantastic teachers: time management skills, passion for subject matter, and internal motivation.

A common misconception about career changers is that they are failures in their previous careers. Not only is this grossly inaccurate, but it is dangerous for any mentor to judge a new teacher in this way. If a mentor has this preconceived notion, it immediately impedes building a positive relationship with a new teacher.

It is important to understand why people change careers into teaching. Recruiting New Teachers (The Teacher Center, 2004), a nonprofit organization, provides five reasons why people change careers into teaching:

1. To give back. Successful mid-career professionals often want to "pay back" that great teacher or the educational community that helped them achieve academically and personally.

2. To put experience to use. Mid-career changers want to bring various experience to the classroom, such as expertise developed in another career, maturity, negotiating skills, or parenting experience.
3. To change the meaning of "work." Mid-career changers often go into teaching for the opportunity to mentor and interact with young people, to get closer to their community, and to awaken young minds.
4. To follow one successful career with another. Individuals with experience in the military, the Peace Corps, and other careers have the drive and commitment to be successful teachers.
5. To share knowledge and passion. Mid-career changers combine the enthusiasm and dedication of new teachers with deep understanding of subjects such as mathematics, science, literature, or technology.

Recognizing the potential of career changers is the first step for a mentor in giving guidance. By embracing the previous experiences of the new teacher, mentors can encourage mentees to tap into a knowledge base that has the potential to transform their teaching. Ben's accolade as a new teacher is an example of how his previous career has had a positive impact on his classroom and also the classrooms around him.

Chain of Command

Jill graduated with a degree in elementary education from a small college in Nebraska. She never thought she could afford the costs of attending a university until she enlisted in the local National Guard. This gave her the opportunity to complete her degree while serving her country at various times throughout the year.

Upon graduation, her unit was called to serve overseas for eighteen months. She was more than proud to serve knowing it would make her a better person when she eventually secured a teaching position. In fact, her duties included a component of teaching English to local citizens in the country where she was deployed. At the end of the eighteen months, her unit was reassigned to another country where she then served for twelve more months.

"I didn't see my service in the National Guard at all as an interruption to my career. It really helped me to solidify my knowledge about teaching and gave me a totally different perspective on life. Although I was never in a combat zone, I enjoyed the team building experiences and camaraderie of my fellow soldiers. It was a terrific experience. I looked forward to bringing back my experiences to the classroom."

After Jill's military service, she immediately began applying for teaching positions. She was offered three positions in schools that she liked. She selected the school that was equipped with several high-tech computer labs and other cutting-edge teaching tools that were available for all teachers to use. This school also had an extensive new-teacher induction program that offered a lot of assistance to beginning instructors.

"The school was fantastic. I was afraid that I would teach at a school that was not as 'wired' as what my training in the military, and university afforded me. My mentor, Chris, was also a great match, and she spent a good deal of time during the summer helping me with all the things a new teacher needs to know. She had ten years of experience and had already set up her room early in the summer, so she was able to spend some good chunks of time with me."

It wasn't too long before Jill realized that her mentor was being more than helpful. In fact, she was starting to wonder if the advice Chris was giving her was not only a bit too much, but also too narrow in focus. Jill began to see a pattern of suggestion that closely resembled Chris's way of teaching. Jill felt pressure to mimic the way Chris was teaching. Chris turned controlling. If Jill diverged from Chris's plans, Chris scolded her.

"It was actually starting to get kind of frightening to hear her comments and thoughts about how I should conduct my lessons. After being in the military for almost three years, I really thought I would enter a career that gave me a lot more independence and freedom to select my own teaching strategies.

"Although I was closely following the school district curriculum and state goals, Chris would often give me her set of lesson plans to execute with the students along with very specific methods to follow. I wasn't quite sure how to handle this as I thought she was really infringing on my space.

"Even though she was mostly friendly and casual about it, nonetheless, I often felt compelled to follow her directions because when I didn't, she would be disappointed or sometimes angry."

Jill eventually contacted the director of the new-teacher induction program who had originally set up the mentor/teacher pairs. She was concerned that the director would not handle the situation professionally, and that an intervention with Chris would not go over so well. The director said he would set up a meeting for the three of them to discuss how best to resolve the situation so that Jill would feel more comfortable working with Chris as the year progressed.

QUESTIONS FOR FURTHER THOUGHT

1. Although mentors rarely try to consciously "clone" themselves with their mentee, it can often appear to be that way in the eyes of the new teacher. How should Jill handle this situation?
2. What are some specific issues a mentor may need to beware of when working with a former military person? Does this change the relationship in any ways?
3. If a new teacher/mentor pair is not working out, what kind of "exit" procedures should an induction program provide in order to reassign a new mentor?
4. What is the fine line for a mentor between helping out and forcing too much help? Can this line be definitive, or is this aspect of mentoring too subjective or contextually dependent?

ANOTHER LOOK

People with military experience often make great teachers. Jill is clearly an enthusiastic teacher who wants to succeed in all that she does in the classroom. Jill's previous experience is certainly not the norm for teachers new to the profession.

Mentors need to be aware that a new teacher with military experience is a highly qualified candidate for a teaching position. The results of a Walzer (2005) survey of 875 principals across the nation who supervised teachers with military experience speak for themselves; "Sixty-seven percent . . . said [teachers with military experience] were better prepared to teach than their peers; 72 percent said ex-military teachers dealt better with parents."

So why do ex-military teachers have such a high success rate in the classroom? The answer is based on the qualities that have led to successful military careers. Here is what a mentor can expect of a new teacher with military training:

- "determination and discipline, maturity and experience" (Walzer, 2005)
- "a refusal to surrender, an armor of self-confidence" (Walzer, 2005)
- "When there is a concern or a problem, they know the channels to go through" (Walzer, 2005)
- The ability to multitask (Walzer, 2005)
- Eric Combs, an assistant principal in Ohio, explains that "most people in the military know how to work in an austere environment and a hostile environment and to be project-oriented and to get the task done." (Miller, 2009)
- The military is a culturally diverse environment. Ex-military teachers are sensitive to diverse communities in schools. (Walzer, 2005)
- Leadership skills (Daniels, 2004)
- Motivation (Daniels, 2004)
- Independence tempered with the ability to seek out help when needed (Miller, 2009)

Mentors can better serve the needs of ex-military new teachers when they understand the skill set and qualities that they possess; furthermore, mentors aid the entire educational community by encouraging new teachers to use these skills.

Of course, many new teachers without military experience still have these qualities, but it is important to understand that military men and women come from a background where these qualities are essential for success.

Going Back to the Classroom

Jacob is a teacher with experience in the classroom and in administration. This is his story about the transition back into the classroom after years as an administrator.

"For eleven years I taught in the primary grades at a suburban elementary school. Three years ago, I accepted a position as an assistant principal at an elementary school in another district. During this time, I developed trust among the staff, created consistent discipline policies with students, and built communication with parents.

"In early October our principal had announced his intention to retire at the conclusion of the school year. Within several weeks I was contacted by our district superintendent and offered the position as principal. I had seen the challenges and opportunities which were available to me as an administrator; both he and I were proud of what I accomplished.

"It would be a demanding position but one at which I knew I could excel. I enjoyed my experiences as an administrator, but I did not accept the position as principal. Instead I asked the superintendent if I could be reassigned to a primary classroom.

"I can still remember the expression on his face. I missed the kids, and I loved teaching. I found that as an administrator I no longer had the connection to them which I had as a teacher. I was reassigned as a first-grade teacher within the district, and I have a great amount of respect for school administrators.

"Other administrators told me that I could not take such a demotion, or that I should never degrade myself. I never thought of it as a demotion. I would reply, 'I missed the kids. I loved teaching first grade.' I really wondered why they were even school principals.

"I was reassigned to another school within the district. Before the start of the school year, I received a phone call from our mentor program coordinator. He explained that because my teaching experience was in another school district, I was going to be assigned a mentor. 'You will be an easy one,' he said and gave me the name of my mentor.

"When we first spoke it was over the phone. I explained who I was, where I had taught, and what I had done as an assistant principal. She explained she had recently been tenured as an intermediate teacher within my new building.

"She was rather short over the phone. She was quick to remind me that I was no longer on the 'dark side,' and was delighted that I would now be able to join the union. Initially, I was convinced my new mentor was intimidated at having a 'seasoned' protégé. Nonetheless, I looked forward to being back in the classroom.

"In time I found her to be insecure; I think she felt obligated to prove herself. She needed to prove that she was an exemplary teacher and that she could be a good mentor. She later realized that I was her first protégé. She wanted validation from me. I recognized she had strong teaching traits, but she was also overly sarcastic with her intermediate students.

"I went to her when I thought a student should be referred to for special education services. She said it would be a waste of time, nothing would ever happen anyway. I went to her with my concerns; I thought we can always improve in something. Her harsh response was almost disrespectful."

QUESTIONS FOR FURTHER THOUGHT

1. How did other people's perceptions about Jacob's job change impact his new position? Generally, why did people have the reactions that they did to Jacob's decision to become a classroom teacher again?
2. What could a mentor do to ensure that Jacob's experience in a new school goes smoothly? What would be some things for a mentor to avoid?

3. What were the forces at work that caused Jacob's relationship with his mentor to be strained?
4. What are some strategies that Jacob could use to make his relationship with his mentor more positive?

ANOTHER LOOK

Jacob's situation is a classic case of an experienced educator who does not need a professional mentor. Jacob's ability to teach is never in question. Both the school principal and his assigned mentor recognize that he is highly qualified. So why is he assigned a mentor?

The answer to the question is simple: The district requires teachers new to a school to be assigned a mentor. Rather than assess the situation based on the needs of Jacob, the principal decided to give him a mentor regardless of the fact that the pairing was doomed to failure.

Schools must recognize that experienced teachers new to a district require very little mentoring when it comes to day-to-day practices. What they require is someone to help them navigate the new cultures of a school.

In the event that an unnecessary mentoring pair is established, this pair should be dissolved entirely or the professional relationship should be modified to accommodate the needs of the new teacher.

Crossing International Borders

María, a 25-year-old graduate from a university in Barcelona with a teaching certificate in high school physics, was not able to find a classroom position in her native country of Spain. She read an article in a local education journal that the Department of Human Resources for Chicago Public Schools was conducting interviews in order to recruit and hire teachers to fill positions in math and science at their high schools. One qualification was to be bilingual in both Spanish and English.

"I was quite excited to hear the possibility to live and work in the United States. It was like a dream come true. I gathered my documents and made an appointment with the recruiting advisers. My only concern was taking an English proficiency test. I studied English in Scotland during a six-week summer program but wasn't sure that would be enough as I heard American English was quite different, especially in the cities."

Not only did María do well on the English proficiency test but was met with a great deal of enthusiasm at the interview and was soon offered a position at a near southside Chicago high school. Work permits, visas, and housing arrangements were also provided for her in order to make for a smooth transition. The entire process went quite quickly for María and the other teaching candidates.

"We all met for the first time at the airport in Chicago and lived in group housing provided to us for the orientation. After that they were quite nice to help us find our own housing. I met two other teachers in the program and found a nice apartment about five miles from school.

"I was not expecting it, but I was assigned to a mentor who also taught physics at another high school. He did a great job showing me the curriculum and standards. My only concern was that his school was quite far from mine and could make communicating difficult."

María's classroom was fairly well equipped and up to date in order for her to teach physics. What took her by surprise was not only the large class sizes but the fact that most of the children did not speak English very well. Most came from Chinese homes where Mandarin was the first language, not Spanish, as she had expected.

Soon, she sensed a bit of prejudice not only coming from fellow teachers but also from some of the parents of her students. Whether real or perceived, María often heard comments from students and teachers that her "European" style of teaching was contrary to their expectations. Several people mentioned to her that this is "not the way we teach in America."

"I wasn't quite sure whom to turn to. My mentor seemed to always be too busy to get together to discuss these issues. He could only help me with curriculum matters, not the strained interactions with other people.

"The parents began to question my skills as a physics teacher and whether their children would be prepared for college entrance exams. I had a great deal of difficulty during parent/teacher conferences as neither I nor the parents spoke English as a first language.

"The only help I got about this matter from my mentor was when he gave me a one-page list of phrases often used when meeting with parents that he said I could memorize ahead of time and thus sound like I really knew English well. It was rather insulting for me and only made matters worse."

As the year progressed, other issues began to surface. Although classroom discipline was not a major factor, María sensed that her status as an immigrant was problematic for parents and students even though most of her students came from families also new to America.

She finished the school year but returned to Spain in June with mixed emotions about her whole experience. During her exit interview she expressed thanks for having the opportunity to work and live in America but wasn't sure what other kinds of preparation could have helped to make her teaching experience run smoother.

QUESTIONS FOR FURTHER THOUGHT

1. What are some of the factors that the recruiting team should ask, if not consider, before hiring teachers from another country?
2. Would it have been better to match up María with another teacher in her building who may not have been a curriculum expert in physics but would have at least known enough about the school culture and climate to help her out with multicultural issues?
3. Was her lack of American English skills the core of the problem?
4. What are the unique issues of monitoring the progress of international teachers who are first-time teachers in the United States?

ANOTHER LOOK

Teachers with María's qualifications are in high demand in many public school systems, but many school systems do not hire teachers from other countries. "In 2000, however, Chicago Public Schools (CPS) recruited forty-four teaching candidates from twenty-two different countries. The candidates were required to pass a written and oral exam in English as well as engage in a series of interviews with CPS principals. Those that passed the exams and had successful interviews entered a six week orientation dedicated to training these teachers for a position in a public school" (McCoubrey, 2001).

In addition, "a temporary teaching certificate was issued by the Illinois State Board of Education for the first four years of teaching. After four years, the teachers were responsible for completing requirements for a standard certificate. Visas issued to these teachers were valid for six years, so all candidates had an opportunity to complete their standard certification" (McCoubrey, 2001).

If teachers were deemed well qualified for continued employment, "CPS then had the option to sponsor candidates for permanent visas. These special, H1-B visas were usually reserved for higher education and advanced technology jobs; this was the first time that public school teachers were offered the same opportunity" (McCoubrey, 2001).

"The H1-B visa has specific stipulations. Any applicant for the H1-B visa must have specialized knowledge in a specialty occupation as well as these other professional qualifications:

- The individual must have at least a bachelor's degree in a specific field, but might be able to substitute three years in the field as the equivalent of one year of college. Typically, professors or teachers will meet this requirement because it is already part of the required background for their employment.
- If a teacher requires licensing to teach at a particular school, the teacher will need to show possession of a license or present

documentation from the licensing board that the teacher has met all of the requirements for the license and the only thing holding up issuance of the license is possession of a visa or social security number" (Siskund Susser Bland, 2009).

Clearly these requirements for immigrant teachers match up with many states' certification requirements for American citizens. Unfortunately, biases still exist toward hiring teachers from abroad, but the simple fact is that school districts are struggling to hire highly qualified teachers.

Many school districts hire underqualified, noncertified adults to teach courses. Many states allow school districts to fill open positions with adults with substitute certification. Often these substitute certificates are awarded to college graduates who lack teacher training.

Perhaps looking to international neighbors will yield highly qualified candidates who can greatly contribute to American schools, but school districts must be prepared to institute effective new-teacher induction and mentorship programs that are specifically designed for these new teachers; otherwise, stories like María's will become the norm as opposed to the exception.

Politics in the Classroom

"It was all pretty exciting. Somehow, in the middle of all the campaigning, I landed a job teaching second grade. I knew I had to make some decisions that my teaching career came first and political activity would definitely be second."

Sue met her mentor about a month before school started. It was just before the 2008 Democratic and Republican party conventions. Her mentor, Jill, equally shared her enthusiasm for "all things political" but also agreed that Sue needed to set her priorities straight as the fall political scene was going to be nothing less than intense; Jill suggested that Sue's second-grade class should be front and center.

"Jill was going to be a great mentor for me. We had a lot in common, not only with our teaching philosophies, but a shared vision of the direction where our country was headed. She gave me lots of cool ideas to help set up my room. We immediately established a text-messaging friendship and corresponded often via e-mails.

"I was really comfortable talking to Jill with quick messages; we were in constant communication. I was amazed at how fast she would respond to my questions with all the concerns I had about my students. I felt I could really let down my guard and inform her about all my ups and downs in the classroom."

But Sue quickly felt that Jill was less than forthcoming about her openness and honesty. Even though Sue felt she was doing a terrific job as a first-year teacher, she was getting comments from other teachers, as well as the curriculum director, that perhaps some of her teaching methods and activities were not in line with the school's philosophy on teaching.

Although she got along with her fellow staff members, Sue began to wonder how they knew what her teaching practices and methods were without them ever being in her classroom. Some of the comments were positive, though many were more like, "Well, Sue, we just don't do things that way here."

"I began to think that private e-mails to my mentor were being copied and forwarded to other staff members. I'm not sure why or if Jill would do that, but I wasn't sure how to approach her. With the fall campaign season coming to a fever pitch, I wanted to involve my students in the election process. I thought second graders would be able to handle the basic concepts. Besides, I had stacks of election materials that I could pass out."

Before long, Sue was getting comments from the principal about her political activities in the classroom. The principal questioned where the election lessons stood with the curriculum goals and objectives, though he had not been in her classroom much that fall. In fact, she thought he was forming many ideas about her classroom techniques but had only made one formal visit in September.

"Could my mentor be 'spying' on me? Was she jealous of my lessons and trying to sabotage my position in the school? I'm not the paranoid type, but somehow I wasn't sure what to do next. Do I confront her or just go easy on the text messaging and e-mails?"

QUESTIONS FOR FURTHER THOUGHT

1. Was Sue correct to think that her mentor was, in fact, a spy and not keeping her e-mails private?
2. Generally speaking, what are the privacy policy issues with sharing staff e-mails? Are they really to be treated like public "postcards" as many contend?
3. How should Sue continue her relationship with her mentor if she feels that her confidence and trust level have been tarnished?

ANOTHER LOOK

Sue's political involvement outside of school is admirable and well within her rights, but there is a fine line between teaching students about the election process and campaigning in her classroom that she does not want to cross. Teaching students about their civic duties as citizens is an appropriate, important activity, but if Sue were to campaign for a candidate or influence the political beliefs of her students, she may be crossing ethical and legal lines that could cost her the teaching job that she loves.

Kathleen Kingsbury (2008) in a *Time* magazine article conveys how fine the line can be between teaching students about democracy and campaigning for (or against) a candidate. Many school districts have policies against displaying campaign signs or wearing campaign buttons. During the 2008 presidential campaign, the New York City teachers' union filed "a temporary restraining order against a district policy that bars teachers from wearing campaign buttons in the city's public schools. The prohibition, union officials argue, is a violation of teachers' First Amendment rights to free speech and political expression."

Many school districts have laws similar to New York City's public schools. According to Ask SAM (2008), in the Winston-Salem/ Forsyth County school system "employees are allowed to endorse candidates as long as it is outside the classroom, on their off-duty time. Teachers can't do this at school. Teachers may (and should) encourage students to be informed about politics. But teachers aren't allowed to endorse a candidate or a political party during class, for instance, or to send notes home to parents in support of a candidate."

In some cases, the line is easy to draw because the actions of the teacher are completely inappropriate. *Time* magazine cites an example of a teacher writing a racial slur about Barack Obama on the blackboard. But what about more hazy issues like a teacher who invites her students to her wedding?

In a San Francisco case, the teacher in question is a lesbian. Does this action promote same-sex marriage, or is it a lesson in acceptance and diversity, or simply a caring teacher wanting her students to celebrate a milestone in her life?

The principal at this school, Liz Jaroflow, explains "that the nuptials were a 'teachable moment' and pointed out that students who did not have parental permission to attend the event had the option of joining another classroom instead. 'It's certainly an issue I would be willing to put my job on the line for,' she said" (Kingsbury, 2008). Clearly this is a polarizing event, but did it cross ethical or legal boundaries?

Some teachers will opt to never discuss political points of view with students, but what about with other teachers? The Higley Unified School District in Arizona punished teachers for using school e-mail to discuss politics.

The teachers wanted "to promote the extension of a seven-year budget override to support their schools—a violation of state education laws and the district's ethics policy." The teachers were sending e-mails to the local newspaper supporting the increase in the budget.

The district chose to take disciplinary action even though "teacher activism like this happens in nearly every district, and it is legal. It is illegal, though, when a teacher utilizes work time, the work place or other district resources to promote a political effort" (Gersema, 2008).

There was a public outcry as well because of the fact that the budget increase would also increase teacher salaries. This conflict of interest made many taxpayers within the district upset.

New teachers may not know the ethics policies put into place by school districts to deter teachers from political activity during the school day. It is up to mentors to redirect inappropriate political activity and to make new teachers aware of political stances that may make waves in the district.

While discussing our nation's political system is an essential part of our school systems, all teachers must consider the ramifications of politicking their personal viewpoints, not only for their own personal job security but because of the impact teachers have on students.

All teachers have a strong influence on their students. We must be careful about how we express and emphasize our personal beliefs, as ours is a place of power in the lives of children.

Power Play

Bob is a physical education instructor in his first year of teaching. He entered his current position with no previous teaching experience. He teaches both physical education and health courses. He began teaching right after college.

"Ever since I was in high school, I have always wanted to be a physical education teacher, but more importantly, I wanted to coach several sports at the high school level. I participated in just about every sport possible in high school but considered wrestling to be my best. I won several state competitions and coached several after-school programs for the local middle school.

"I mentored several freshman wrestlers at my high school and was treated like an adult—almost like an assistant coach, even though I was only a senior in high school. I was highly regarded by the other coaches as a role model for others. I received several scholarships to attend a university that specialized in physical education and coaching."

During his senior year in college, Bob completed many online high school application forms for a teaching position. Because of his stellar recommendations and previous background, he was invited to interview at several high schools.

One high school in particular, where he ultimately was offered and accepted the position, had a very in-depth and thorough review process. This school is a large, suburban high school well known for its highly successful, highly competitive athletics programs.

"I remembered how excited I was when I went for the third and final interview at Lincoln High School. It seemed like the entire coaching staff was there. They asked me far more questions about various coaching positions but hardly anything at all about day-to-day physical education classes.

"When I asked them about the health classes I was expected to teach, they told me not to worry about it as you can just have them read the book and answer questions at the end of the chapter. It was obvious that they were far more interested in filling coaching positions than how I would best handle the PE classes."

Bob accepted the position knowing that he would be assigned a mentor. He knew that he would have to coach sports during all three seasons. His favorite was, of course, wrestling. He felt that he could create an even more winning team based on his previous experiences; he put much time and effort into his coaching duties.

As far as his teaching, Bob's physical education periods went well, but he was struggling with the health classes. He had more than thirty students in a class and had a problem with discipline because he had very little experience with teaching in a classroom setting.

"I went to my mentor, whose roles and responsibilities for guiding me were never really defined. I didn't know how much and how often we were to meet and how to approach him with questions. He was a nice guy but seemed a bit distant.

"When I asked for support and help with my health classes, I never really got a decent or helpful answer. In fact, I was starting to get some criticism with how I was directing the sophomore wrestling team."

Bob soon realized that his mentor was more concerned about his coaching skills than with his classroom success. There appeared to be conflicting philosophies about how to coach the wrestling team, and other coaches had begun to question Bob's methods. This was strange because the athletes were winning more matches that the previous years.

Tensions started to build between Bob and the other coaches. Unfortunately, Bob's mentor was running for the soon-to-be-vacant department chair position, which made things even more awkward.

"I felt that my mentor was actually 'turning' on me in order to show his version of leadership skills in order to impress the school administration. He really wanted to be department chair. He began verbally pushing me around and said he couldn't believe what a horrible job I was doing with coaching the wrestling team. I think he was trying to show what terrific leadership skills he had. The opposite was happening."

In April, Bob informed his mentor and department chair that he did not plan to coach wrestling the next year. He had a total philosophical difference with how to run the team. He was sure that he was doing his best. His already frosty relationship with his mentor became even worse. All of a sudden, all of the other physical education teachers were giving him the cold shoulder.

"I would walk into the coaches offices and everyone turned away. Guys who previously would say hello and ask how things were going stopped talking to me altogether. It was horrible. What made it worse, my mentor said he was going to recommend that I not be hired next year and let go in June."

It became apparent to me that mentors, who I thought were supposed to help and support me, had the power to get me fired. Even though he was considered a fellow teacher, this mentorship thing and his desire to be department chair went to his head. He told me how disappointed he was with me because I no longer wanted to coach wrestling. He then told me how many other people were up for the position, and that they gave the job to me because I showed the most promise.

"He told me how sorry the other coaches were; they felt that they should have hired one of the other candidates. I really wanted to come back again next year, but I was sure that my mentor was going to make sure that I got fired."

Bob found himself in a very lonely place at school, and he had no idea that his mentor could terminate his teaching position. He thought the best thing to do was to start his job search for another school, but he wondered what kind of letters of recommendation he could possibly get from anyone at Lincoln High School. Bob knew that he would soon be leaving on a very low note.

QUESTIONS FOR FURTHER THOUGHT

1. Is Bob's story a fairly typical situation? Are some people hired more for their coaching experience than for their teaching ability?
2. Can Bob's mentor, who is classified as a regular classroom teacher, actually get him terminated from his teaching assignment at the school? Explore the context at your school.
3. Would stating clearly defined roles and duties for mentors have made Bob's situation better? Or is the situation independent from a strong mentoring program?
4. What are some of the misconceptions that Bob may have about the role of his mentor?
5. Was Bob's mentor placing his own career advancement above mentoring Bob?

ANOTHER LOOK

Bob's story brings to the forefront an unfortunate trend of the new-teacher experience: hazing. More and more new teachers report that other staff members in schools are making their first years of teaching miserable.

In 2006 a superintendent in a Chicago-area school videotaped new-teachers' interviews. He then used their answers in a comedic video that he showed during the first days of school. The superintendent would ask fake questions, but he would then edit in the new-teachers' answers to make their answers seem inappropriate or to make them appear incompetent and unintelligent. This sparked debate in the educational community. Some teachers felt that the incident was harmless fun while others, especially the new teachers, were appalled by the behavior of the administrator.

New teachers already have it extremely tough, and this incident is a reminder that some experienced teachers believe that hazing of new teachers is a rite of passage. Effective, compassionate mentors know better, though. Bob's situation is a vivid representation of an experienced teacher who abuses his power. Bob's mentor used his power to sway the opinions of the teachers around them and essentially isolate Bob. Clearly, Bob was negatively affected by this treatment, and the mentor's actions were intentional.

But what happens when the hazing is unintentional—or systemic? Patterson (2005) reflects, "When new teachers consistently experience poorer working conditions than their veteran colleagues, there's a word for that . . . Beginning teachers are often systematically hazed." She further notes "that the new teachers who left the school I focused on almost never did so because of the challenges of teaching, the long hours, or the low pay. They left because they believed that they were in impossible situations in which they would never experience success or career satisfaction."

Bob was set up for failure from the beginning. He was given a course load that he had virtually no experience in, and even though he had a mentor, there was not an effective program in place to help him as a new teacher.

The comments made by other teachers that Bob could "just have them read the book and answer questions at the end of the chapter" is evidence of a throw-them-to-the-wolves type of sentiment. This apathy when it comes to new-teacher induction is extremely harmful to the educator community.

Patterson (2005) makes these recommendations during the hiring process:

> New teachers need not be given easier or better assignments than their veteran peers—although there is reason to believe that this should be the case. But schools should make a concerted effort to make assignments more equitable. To this end, they should:
>
> - Avoid hiring new teachers at the last minute or after the school year has already begun.
> - Create survivable schedules for new teachers by giving them one classroom, no more than two preps, and a mix of freshman and higher-level courses.
> - Foster a supportive environment by locating new teachers' classrooms near those of helpful veteran teachers in their department.
> - Provide new teachers with curriculum binders that hold sample lesson plans, quizzes, and homework assignments.
> - Provide new teachers with adequate books and materials for their students.
> - Give new teachers concrete information regarding departmental standards, expectations, and timelines.

These suggestions, along with helpful, compassionate mentors, will keep new teachers confident and enthusiastic. Here is the story of Harry McDonald, a twenty-five-year teacher out of Kansas:

> McDonald gave up his coveted last-period planning session so that a new teacher who coaches could have it. And he asked to mentor three new biology teachers. As a result, McDonald reports, "Our whole department seems energized with a new spirit of sharing." There has been a lot of talk lately about "healing the breach." (Chase, 1998)

Mr. McDonald is an excellent example of veteran teachers ensuring that new teachers have the best opportunity to succeed. Chase (1998) puts it best by observing that "we would be wise to draw inspiration from Harry McDonald. For while new teachers have always felt overwhelmed, the problems they face today are exponentially greater than the ones we veterans faced 10 or 20 or 30 years ago. To succeed, this new generation of teachers requires greater support from our state and local Associations as well as a willingness among 'elder' colleagues to share our professional expertise and privileges."

Indeed, there is no room in the teacher community for extraneous pressures especially when the unnecessary pressure comes from veteran educators and mentors.

Pushy Parents

"I'm caught right in the middle! Even the parents of my students don't like my mentor and want to intervene. They want the best for the children as well as for me, the new teacher. But my mentor is a disaster and the worst role model I could possibly imagine!"

Such was the dilemma for Nancy, a brand-new seventh-grade social studies teacher at a middle school in Sacramento, California. Part of the new-teacher induction program included four half days to observe mentoring teachers in their classrooms. Nancy had already done two observations of her mentor, Joan, and was all but appalled with what she saw.

"I have never seen the bar set so low and the standards so compromised as I did when I observed my mentor teaching sixth-grade social studies. It was as if she were from another planet. She is way too easy, and keeps saying how she wants me to be just like her! She has boring lectures, allows open notes on tests all of the time, there are no deadlines for homework, and she permits students to collaborate on tests.

"Does this sound like learning? On top of this, her entire class is based on the textbook, and there are very few activities. I don't like how she teaches. I think she's really given up. Sadly, she is only thirty-five years old. I'm really feeling desperate. Is this what teaching is really like? Is this what other teachers are like?"

Although Nancy knew that Joan was not the best model of a teacher, several of her parents even complained that this assigned mentor was not going to work out. Nancy's mentor had a reputation in the school community of being a bad teacher.

When the parents found out that their child's brand-new teacher was asked to work closely with Joan, they went straight to the principal, bypassing Nancy. Because of tenure laws, the parents knew that Joan was "here to stay," but they wanted Nancy to be reassigned to another mentor for the good of their children.

"You know it's not a good sign when even the parents complain about your mentor. Had I known they were going to express their concerns to the principal before even asking me, I would have certainly stepped in. But I thought, well, let them get the ball rolling and see if we can get the situation fixed before the school year moves on.

"My biggest concern was how to keep Joan's feelings from getting hurt. My worst fear was that the parents would come to me and ask me for comments about Joan's teaching methods (or lack thereof) and use that to build a case for termination against her."

"I wanted to make an appointment with the principal and clear up things before they got ugly, but this was already draining enough energy from me, and I started to lose focus with the real task at hand, teaching my seventh-grade students."

QUESTIONS FOR FURTHER THOUGHT

1. How should Nancy discuss the situation when she meets with the principal? What kinds of documentation should she bring to the meeting?
2. Should she approach her mentor, Joan, and lay the facts on the table?

3. What kinds of strategies should Nancy implement to keep the parents at bay?

4. What's the worst thing that she could do to make matters even more complicated?

ANOTHER LOOK

There are a number of issues that present themselves in Nancy's story. She clearly does not have trust in her mentor, Joan, nor does she think that observing Joan will be helpful. Nancy may have a larger problem than her relationship with her mentor, though; she is in danger of destroying her relationship with the parents of the children she teaches.

It is Nancy's responsibility to build trust with the parents as well as establish herself as an independent, active participant in her own classroom and employment at the school. Allowing parents to advocate for a direct change in her new-teacher induction, even if the change is positive, sends a message that she has relinquished control to these parents.

"Sometimes parents require new teachers to earn their trust, recalls Mike Benevento (Upper Saddle River, New Jersey). 'Parents have a hard time with first-year teachers. They view us as experimenting with their kid. If you show them you really care, then they are supportive'" (U.S. ED, 2004).

Indeed, Nancy's parents felt that the 'experimentation' with their children was too risky because Joan was involved. Rather than discussing the parents' concerns directly with them, Nancy adopted a passive approach to the situation. Because Nancy saw Joan's mentorship as a problem too, she was content to let the parents work it out for her.

Immediately, any trust that the parents had in Nancy to navigate this difficult situation had been lost. If these parents thought that Nancy could handle the problem on her own, they would have gone directly to her, not over her head to the principal.

This type of parent behavior is common for the new teacher to experience. Often, parents will go directly to a principal or other administrator before contacting the new teacher. It is a commonly held belief by parents that new teachers are not equipped to handle the big issues that may arise in the classroom. This is a stereotype that Nancy must destroy immediately.

Here are some tips on how to develop an active, trusting relationship with parents. All teachers can benefit from these ideas, but they are especially important for new teachers. Implementing these strategies with the help of a mentor is suggested as it provides an opportunity for new teachers and mentors to discuss the role of parents in their classroom.

- Write a newsletter or develop ways to get parents involved in the classroom on a regular basis. A first-grade teacher may implement a system where a parent visits the classroom to read to the class every Friday afternoon. A high school teacher may write a blog on the school website to describe what students are learning in chemistry.
- Provide parents with a specific, hands-on responsibility at home. A third-grade teacher can urge parents to be a word wizard—parents have the opportunity to work on the meanings and spellings of words in a weekly list. For older students, teachers can incorporate assignments that require students to have discussions with their parents. A social studies teacher could have her students interview parents about the ways that their childhoods were different than the students'.
- "Address parents' concerns head on. If you are taking a pedagogical approach that raises questions, work to show parents the benefits of your methods and explain your reasoning to them" (U.S. ED, 2004) Parents are often receptive to discussions about the philosophical approach that teachers have to their classroom practice. Promote an understanding of the methods being used in the classroom. Share with parents specific examples of the success of these methods.

- Take advantage of open house to show parents all of the ways that they can be involved. This is the perfect opportunity to discuss the role of parents in the education of their children. If your school does not have a forum for this, be active and contact parents at the beginning of the year with phone calls, e-mails, newsletters, or even home visits.
- Always leave time for parents to ask questions. If there is a question that you cannot answer, politely explain that you do not know or that the answer requires further thought. Emphasize that you will contact parents as soon as possible to let them know the answer.
- Emphasize the myriad ways that parents can contact you, and always be appreciative when parents reach out to you. Provide parents with your phone number, e-mail address, and any other applicable information for contacting you at school.

Doug Fiore asserts that providing contact information outside of the school building can have positive results: "experience has shown us over and over again that providing parents with your home phone number does not increase phone calls to your home. Let's face it, if a parent wants to contact you at home, they will often find a way to do so. Providing parents with your phone number is a tremendous way to demonstrate that you care and that you want to be accessible. For most parents, that will be the clear implication when you give out your phone number.

"In reality, the opposite reaction from what you'd expect usually occurs. Parents don't call you at home because they assume that you already get lots of calls at home. They recognize how much you care, and they are often more willing to wait and talk to you at school" (Hopkins, 2007).

Of course, your comfort level will dictate whether you decide to use Fiore's strategy, but it is interesting to understand the dynamic at play. The gesture increases trust, and this trust leads to respect. If you don't want to give out your phone number, consider other ways to make a gesture that increases trust.

- But—also set boundaries. Always be polite and professional when interacting with parents, but be a self-advocate when it comes to your time. Parents need to know that you care about their children, but they must also understand that you are not on call twenty-four hours a day.

RECOGNIZING ABILITY

Although many would say being confined to a wheelchair is a disability, Jeffrey never thought of himself as physically handicapped. He has always been quite active in school and community activities. He always wanted to give back to society and decided that being a teacher would be a perfect opportunity to show the world that he could overcome any challenges.

"Throughout high school and college, I worked hard to help make sure that public institutions were following the laws set forth to provide accommodation and access for people with disabilities. The university I attended could easily be considered a role model for providing not only physical access to all areas on campus, but a thoughtful and understanding faculty to help all students reach their full potential, especially during the student teaching term. My practicum experience was outstanding as I observed and worked in a second-grade classroom."

Jeffrey was looking forward to starting his first year of teaching and working with his mentor, Cheryl. They were scheduled to meet one week before school started, but an unexpected illness prevented her from meeting Jeffrey and starting the school year. She would not start school until the fourth week but insisted on being Jeffrey's mentor.

The director of the induction program asked the other mentors to pitch in and help Jeffrey during the first four weeks of school until Cheryl came back. Although not ideal, it was an appropriate temporary solution.

"Everyone was so helpful. The kids were terrific, and the parents more than eager to help as volunteers with my reading and math groups. I had some limited contact with Cheryl who tried her best to help out, but it was difficult for us to communicate. The other teachers filled in nicely during her absence."

Cheryl returned in October and almost immediately felt compelled to "undo" what Jeffrey had started. She said she was sorry not to have been present during the first month of school but made many suggestions to Jeffrey about his teaching methods. Most of the strategies Cheryl suggested were contrary to his style.

He had a comfortable relationship with his class, but Cheryl all but said, "You're doing this all wrong and we need to make some major repairs." Needless to say, Jeffrey was unexcited about her return. What made matters worse was when Jeffrey heard Cheryl make a comment to another teacher that she couldn't believe the school would hire a teacher in a wheelchair.

"I was really shocked to hear her comments and negativity directed at me. I knew she was upset about the fact that she had a late start at a critical time in the school year, but felt she was taking it out on me. I knew I was a strong person and just reminded myself that as a teacher, you simply close the classroom door and it's just you and the students.

"You're in charge, and the rest of the world can't interfere with your teaching. I tried my best to resolve the not-so-good situation but decided to do the best I could to get along with my mentor. It was yet another challenge I felt I could handle."

QUESTIONS FOR FURTHER THOUGHT

1. What are some of the federal protection laws for employees, as well as students, with disabilities?
2. Should the school have assigned another mentor for Jeffrey knowing that Cheryl was not able to start on day one? Were "fill-ins" an OK solution?

3. What are some strategies that new teachers might use when their mentor is overbearing and too "bossy" in the relationship?
4. What are some suggestions for screening teachers before deciding if they should become mentors? What are some ways in which the selection process could be improved in order to screen out potential problems?

ANOTHER LOOK

It is unfortunate that Jeffrey and his mentor, Cheryl, have not been able to establish a strong collegial relationship. A substantial impediment to gaining each other's trust is Cheryl's attitude about Jeffrey's disability. She has prequalified him as a man who cannot effectively teach children based on the fact that he uses a wheelchair. It may be possible that Cheryl's criticism of his teaching is unfairly connected to his physical disability.

In order to be an effective mentor, Cheryl needs to understand that Jeffrey may need to use alternative instructional techniques, but that his style of teaching is just as valid as anyone else's. In some cases, Jeffrey may even have distinct advantages over other teachers.

This idea is illuminated in Wills's (2009) article about four excellent educators, all of whom have had to overcome obstacles in their careers as teachers. Amanda Trei, Tricia Downing, Gary LeGates, and Wendy Shugol are all successful teachers who happen to have physical disabilities.

Trei was in a serious car accident when she was a teenager. Her lower body is paralyzed, and she uses a wheelchair. She does not see this as a problem when it comes to teaching young children in her special education class.

In fact, she says, "I have a one-up on anybody who can walk, because I can see what my students need, and I can see the struggles they're going to face. Somebody who isn't disabled—they can read about it, they can watch it, but if they never live through it, they never really know" (Wills, 2009).

Tricia Downing is a competitive athlete and an internship coordinator at a Denver magnet high school. An iron-man triathlete, she is the first paraplegic woman to compete in the world-class event. Her outlook is much the same as Trei's: "'Sometimes, students get stuck in their teenage world, where everything's a crisis,' she says. 'I've been able to get across to students that the world is bigger than their problems. My message is that life is full of challenges, but if you're willing to try to overcome them, you can find the resources within yourself'" (Wills, 2009).

Gary LeGates's story, like that of Trei and Downing's, is simply extraordinary. LeGates started teaching in the late 1970s despite considerable challenges in getting hired. He says, "People were afraid to hire a blind person. I think they were afraid I wouldn't be able to handle the classroom situation."

Not only has he been able to handle the classroom, but LeGates has left a lasting legacy. Reflecting on LeGates's retirement, Principal John Seaman, whose son was a student of LeGates's, says, "I'm convinced that our students have gained an understanding that having an obvious handicap does not preclude someone from being a professional and an intellectual. We will miss him as an influence" (Wills, 2009).

LeGates reports, though, that schools are still not open to the possibility of a blind person being a successful, competent teacher, especially with the new challenges facing educators today.

An important aspect of these teachers' jobs is their role as advocate for students with disabilities. Wendy Shugol, an elementary school teacher with cerebral palsy, explains that "she pushes other teachers to let disabled students decide whether to try something, rather than deciding for them. 'I find my nondisabled counterparts making judgments about students based on what the kids look like,' she says. Years ago, she successfully lobbied for the physical disabilities department to offer more demanding courses such as algebra and physics, and for the school to offer late busing for her students so they could stay for extra help or participate in clubs" (Wills, 2009).

Effective mentors will understand that new teachers with disabilities have just as much to give to their schools as their able-bodied counterparts. Mentors of new teachers with disabilities should not ignore the disabilities of their protégés; rather, they should understand that this facet of their life can be enriching to those around them.

References

Ask SAM. Illegal sign-posting, teachers and politics, waiters off the clock, new flashing-yellow arrow on traffic signal. *Winston-Salem Journal.* (2008, September 24). Accessed March 20, 2009, from http://www2.journalnow .com/content/2008/sep/24/ask-sam/community-askSAM/

Boreen, J., Niday, D., Potts, J., and Johnson, M. (2009). Mentoring beginning teachers. Portland, ME: Stenhouse Publishers.

Bottomley, L. (2007). Setting boundaries. Retrieved April 20, 2009, from http://web1.msue.msu.edu/cyf/youth/mentor/downloads/resources/ SettingBoundariesInMentoringRelationships.pdf.

Chase, Bob. (1998, November). A new deal for teachers. *NEA Today.* Retrieved on March 7, 2009, from http://findarticles.com/p/articles/mi_ qa3617/is_199811/ai_n8822937.

Daniels, Lilly. (2004, April 29). Teachers to troops: Service after the military. Retrieved March 10, 2009, from http://www.navy.mil/search/display .asp?story_id=13027.

Finkelstein, L. M. and Poteet, M. L. (2007). Best practices in workplace formal mentoring programs. In T. Allen & L. Eby (eds.), *The Blackwell Handbook of Mentoring* (pp. 345-368). Indianapolis, IN: Wiley-Blackwell Press.

Gersema, Emily. Higley teachers' campaigning breaking laws. *The Arizona Republic.* (2008, October 24). Accessed March 20, 2009 from http://www .azcentral.com/community/gilbert/articles/2008/10/24/20081024gr -husdviolation1024-ON.html.

Hopkins, Gary. (2007). *Wire side chat: Dealing with difficult parents.* Retrieved January 25, 2009, from http://www.education-world.com/a_ issues/chat/chat111.shtml.

Kapos, S. (2007, January 15). Secret weapon: a young mentor. *Crain's Chicago Business* 30(3), 23–26. Retrieved April 23, 2009, from MasterFILE Premier database.

Kingsbury, Kathleen. Classroom politics: Should teachers endorse a candidate? *Time.* (2008, October 15). Accessed March 20, 2009, from http://www.time.com/time/nation/ article/0,8599,1850598,00.html.

McCoubrey, Scott. Recruiting teachers from abroad. *Techniques.* (2001, May 1). Accessed December 29, 2008, from http://www.accessmylibrary.com/coms2/summary_0286-10822238_ITM.

Miller, Amanda. (2009). Be a teacher by fall. Retrieved March 10, 2009, from http://www.airforcetimes.com/careers/second_careers/military_start_teaching_070208/.

Patterson, Mary. (2005, May). Hazed! Educational Leadership 62(8). Retrieved on March 8, 2009, from ERIC.

Siskund Susser Bland. The ABC's of immigration: Visa options for teachers. Accessed March 26, 2009, from http://www.visalaw.com/04jun1/2jun104.html.

The Teacher Center. (2004). Alternative certification for "career changers" and recent college graduates. Retrieved December 23, 2008, from http://www.theteachercenter.org/.

U.S. Department of Education. (2004). Survival guide for new teachers: Working with new parents. Retrieved January 25, 2009, from http://www.ed.gov/teachers/become/about/survivalguide/parent.html.

University of Minnesota, Counseling and Consulting Services. (2008). Mentorship training. Retrieved April 28, 2009, from www.ucs.umn.edu/documents/MentorshipTrainingTemplate_000.ppt*New Teacher/General Info/altern_cert.asp.*

Walzer, Philip. (2005, October 5). Study: Ex-military often make better teachers. *The Virginia-Pilot.* Retrieved March 10, 2009, from http://www.redorbit.com/news/education/261257/study_exmilitary_often_make_better_teachers.

Wills, Denise K. The advantages of disadvantages. *Edutopia.* Retrieved March 20, 2009, from http://www.edutopia.org/disabled-teachers.

About the Authors

Brandon Geuder is a high school English teacher at his alma mater, Deerfield High School in Deerfield, Illinois. He earned his B.A. from Illinois Wesleyan University in Bloomington, Illinois, with a degree in English literature and writing. Becoming an English teacher was a natural fit for Brandon as he was passionate about the language arts as well as teaching and learning. He earned his master's degree in curriculum and instruction from National-Louis University in Wheeling, Illinois. This allowed him to explore topics such as feedback, assessment, technology in the classroom, and new-teacher mentorship. He resides in Libertyville, Illinois, with his wife, Kelly.

Richard E. Lange is an adjunct faculty member at National-Louis University, Chicago, Illinois, and a staff development Consultant for the Center for Talent Development, Northwestern University, Evanston, Illinois. He holds a B.A. from Carthage College, Kenosha, Wisconsin; an M.Ed. from National-Louis University, Evanston; and an M.S. from Northern Illinois University, DeKalb, Illinois. He is an education consultant to more than thirty school districts in five states and Germany, Switzerland, Hong Kong, and Singapore. He has done education consulting for the Swiss Department of Education in Zurich and serves as a member of numerous new-teacher induction and mentoring task force groups for national organizations. He recently coauthored a chapter in *An Anthology for Researchers, Policy Makers, and Practitioners* titled "Teacher Induction Policies at National and State Levels." He continues to take education leaders on tours to Washington, D.C., to visit legislators to discuss policy issues and advocate for meeting the needs of today's children.

Scott Scafidi is currently the assistant principal at Winston Campus-Elementary School in Palatine, Illinois. Scott was the assistant principal at Pleasant Hill Elementary School, Palatine. He taught social studies and language arts for grades 6–8 at MacArthur Middle School in Prospect Heights, Illinois. He holds a bachelor of arts in history from the University of Illinois, Champaign-Urbana with a minor in secondary education. Scott earned a master of science in education in educational administration from Northern Illinois University. Scott lives with his wife, Laurie, and German shorthaired pointer, Marshall, in Mundelein, Illinois.

DATE DUE

HIGHSMITH

YOUR FAMILY TREE

DNA: Window to the Past

by Jim Ollhoff

Visit us at
www.abdopublishing.com

Published by ABDO Publishing Company, 8000 West 78th Street, Suite 310, Edina, MN 55439.
Copyright ©2011 by Abdo Consulting Group, Inc. International copyrights reserved in all
countries. No part of this book may be reproduced in any form without written permission from
the publisher. ABDO & Daughters™ is a trademark and logo of ABDO Publishing Company.

Printed in the United States of America, North Mankato, Minnesota
052010
092010

 PRINTED ON RECYCLED PAPER

Editor: John Hamilton
Graphic Design: Sue Hamilton
Cover Design: John Hamilton
Cover Photo: Getty Images
Interior Photos: AP-pgs 7, 9, 16, 17 & 20; Corbis-pg 6; FamilyTreeDNA-pg 26; Getty Images-pg 1;
iStockphoto-pgs 3, 8, 10, 11, 12, 14, 18, 22, 23, 24, 25, 27, 28 & 29; Photo Researchers-pgs 5, 6 & 13;
Thinkstock-pgs 4, 15, 19, 21, 31 & 32; U.S. National Library of Medicine-pg 22.

Library of Congress Cataloging-in-Publication Data

Ollhoff, Jim, 1959-
  DNA : window to the past / Jim Ollhoff.
    p. cm. -- (Your family tree)
  Includes index.
  ISBN 978-1-61613-462-4
  1. Genetic genealogy--Juvenile literature. I. Title.
  CS21.O54 2011
  929'.1072--dc22
                      2009050808

Contents

Genetic Genealogy 4

Famous DNA Discoveries...6

What is DNA?...10

How is DNA tested?..14

DNA Testing in Genetic Genealogy..18

Deep Ancestry: When Genes Mutate...22

Deep Ancestry: Haplogroups...24

Your Genealogical Journey..28

Glossary..30

Index..32

Genetic Genealogy

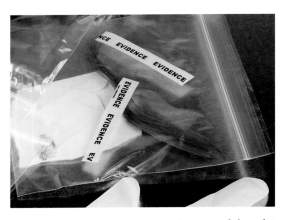

Above: DNA can be used to identify criminals, as well as to find a person's ancestors.

Adetective scours the crime scene. A bank vault is open, the money and jewels gone. As the detective ducks under a low-hanging door frame, his expert eyes spot a piece of evidence. "We have our bank robber!" he exclaims, pulling out a hair stuck in the door frame. "DNA!"

Scenes like this happen every day on television. DNA, our genetic building blocks, can be used to identify criminals. But DNA can also be used to give us genealogical information. This is a new field called genetic genealogy. It's easy and fun, and we don't have to dig up our ancestors to do it!

Testing our DNA can do two things for your genealogy project. It can trace your lineage, and in doing so find other people, such as cousins, who share your ancestors. The second thing it can do is reveal your haplogroup, or ancient ancestry. This allows you to see where your ancient forbearers lived and migrated.

Above: The genetic building blocks of DNA can be used to trace your lineage. Through DNA testing, it's possible to find other people, such as cousins, who share your common ancestors.

Famous DNA Discoveries

Below: DNA testing on an arrow thought to be made from Captain Cook's leg bone was probably made from an antler or a sea mammal bone.

Where is the body of Christopher Columbus? Two places have long claimed to hold the last remains of the famous explorer: a cathedral in Spain, and a lighthouse tomb in the Dominican Republic, an island in the Caribbean Sea. Geneticists extracted DNA from the remains of Columbus's brother Diego, who is buried in Spain. When they compared Diego's DNA to DNA from bodies at the two burial sites, they found a match in the cathedral. Christopher Columbus is buried in Spain.

British explorer Captain James Cook died in Hawaii in 1779. In 1824, Hawaiian King Kamehameha gave an arrow to a British doctor. The king claimed it was made from Captain Cook's bone. It has been displayed at a museum in Australia ever since. However, in 2004, DNA testing proved the arrow was not made from Captain Cook's bone. In fact, it wasn't even a human bone.

DNA testing on bone fragments proved Christopher Columbus's remains are in Spain.

One of the oldest skeletons ever found in England is called "Cheddar Man." It was found in an area called Cheddar Gorge, in Somerset, England. Scientists who tested the age of the skeleton discovered that Cheddar Man lived in the area around 7150 BC. DNA testing of modern-day people found three descendants of Cheddar Man who lived just a few miles from where the skeleton was found. That is an old neighborhood!

Above: Many people in Ireland and Scotland are descendants of the Irish king, Niall Noigiallach.

One of the greatest Irish kings was Niall Noigiallach, known as "Niall of the Nine Hostages." He lived in the 400s AD, and led many raids on the Roman Empire. He has many descendants throughout the land, especially in Ireland. Even in neighboring Scotland today, Y-chromosome DNA testing reveals that about 10 percent of men carry his gene. Between 2 and 3 million men in the world today are probably descended from the king.

People in a remote Chinese village called Liqian, on the edge of the Gobi Desert, have always wondered about their ancestry. Many of the people have traditional western features—even blonde hair—mixed with traditional Chinese features. In the 1950s, historians began to piece together stories of a lost Roman legion. There were stories in the Chinese records detailing a battle against "foreign mercenaries" fighting in a style that sounded like a Roman army tactic. Historians wondered if Roman soldiers founded Liqian in about 53 BC. Residents of Liqian had their DNA tested, and in 2007 geneticists revealed that they had no apparent European ancestry. The mystery continues.

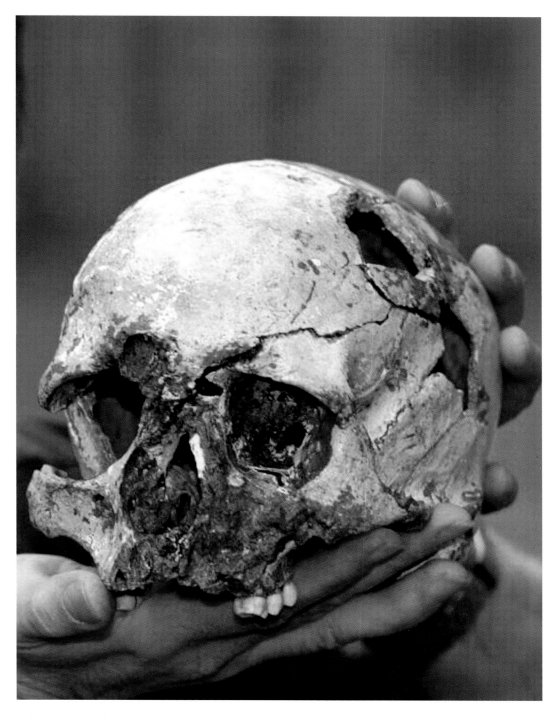

Above: One of the oldest skeletons ever found in England is called "Cheddar Man." DNA testing discovered living descendants of this 9,000-year-old man.

What is DNA?

Below: Our genes tell the body what color to make our eyes, hair, and skin.

Did you ever wonder why your eyes are the color they are? Or why your nose or ears are shaped in a particular way? Or why you are short or tall? It is because of the information in your genes.

A gene is a small unit of information that tells the body what to do. Each person has over 30,000 different genes. Some people have a gene for brown eyes, some have a gene for blue eyes, others for green eyes. Our genes tell the body what color to make our hair and what color to make our skin. Sometimes genes go haywire, and we get a gene that gives us a disease.

Genes aren't the only things that make us who we are. Our environment and experiences also tell our body what to do. So, a child might have a gene to be tall, but if the child is undernourished, he or she will never grow to be tall. There is a complicated relationship between our environment and our genes.

Genes tell our body what to do. But environment also plays a part. A person may have genes to be tall, but if that person is undernourished, he or she will never be tall.

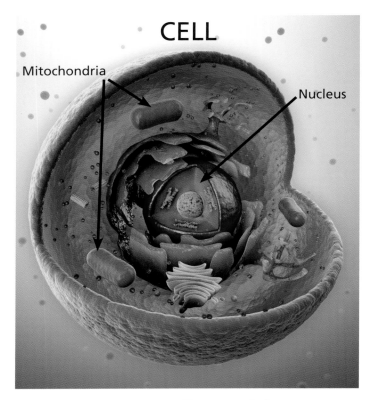

CELL

Mitochondria

Nucleus

Above: DNA is found in most cells in the body. It is found in each cell's nucleus and mitochondria.

All the genes for our entire body are carried on structures called chromosomes. Humans have 23 pairs of chromosomes, which carry all the information we need. We get these chromosomes from our parents—half from our mother and half from our father. That's why we have some of the same traits as our parents and grandparents.

Genes and chromosomes are made up of an organic chemical called <u>d</u>eoxyribo<u>n</u>ucleic <u>a</u>cid, or DNA. It is found in most cells in the body. It is found in the cell nucleus and also in a cell structure called the mitochondria.

Scientists can measure two sets of DNA to see if they match, like fingerprints. For example, they can look at the DNA of a known bank robber and the DNA found in a human hair at a bank crime scene. If the DNA matches, it means that the hair came from the head of the known bank robber.

Everyone's DNA is different (except for identical twins). But you and your relatives share several DNA similarities, which can be tested for and compared.

HUMAN CHROMOSOMES

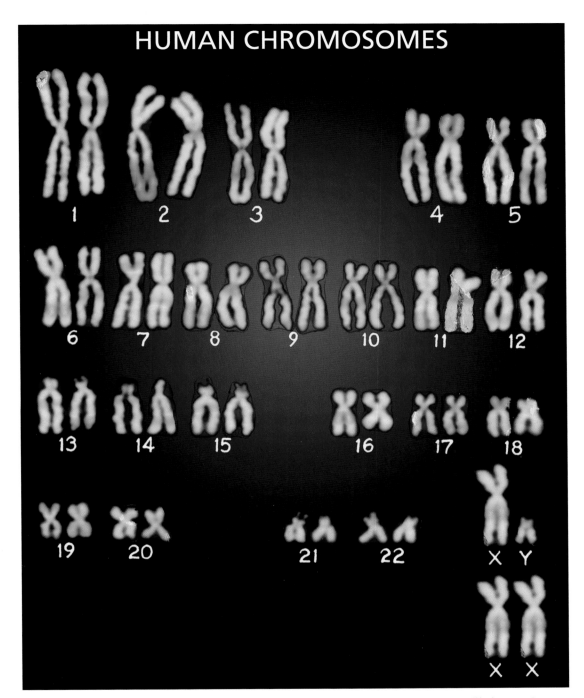

Above: Humans have 23 pairs of chromosomes. The 23rd chromosome will determine if the person is a male or female. Males have an XY chromosome. Females have an XX chromosome.

How is DNA Tested?

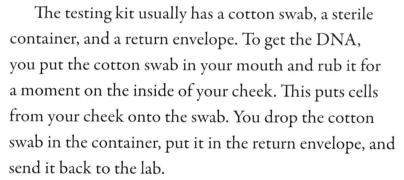

The process of DNA testing is very simple. First, you choose a company that will do the testing. You contact them, and they send you a testing kit. The most basic test is called a 12-marker test, which tests 12 specific areas of a chromosome. A more advanced test is the 37-marker test, which examines more of the DNA for a more accurate reading. Some companies test even more markers. The cost of a testing kit starts at about $100 and goes up from there.

Above: A cotton swab is used to collect DNA.

The testing kit usually has a cotton swab, a sterile container, and a return envelope. To get the DNA, you put the cotton swab in your mouth and rub it for a moment on the inside of your cheek. This puts cells from your cheek onto the swab. You drop the cotton swab in the container, put it in the return envelope, and send it back to the lab.

Some companies will send you a piece of chewing gum. This puts your saliva into the gum, which will be extracted by the company. Some companies use a mouthwash. It's possible to extract DNA from hair, but it's rather expensive, so almost no one does it for genealogy purposes.

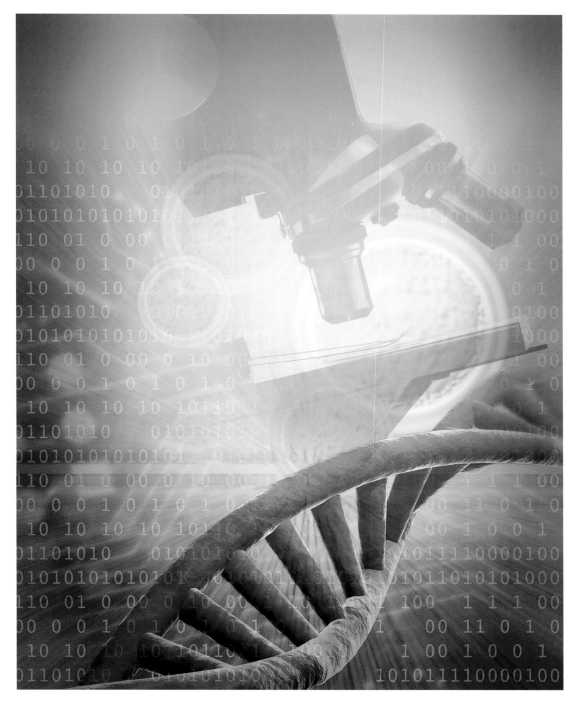

Above: DNA testing is very simple. The most basic test is called a 12-marker test, which tests 12 specific areas of a chromosome. A more advanced test is the 37-marker test.

Right: When DNA is received, a technician will extract the DNA and gather the data.

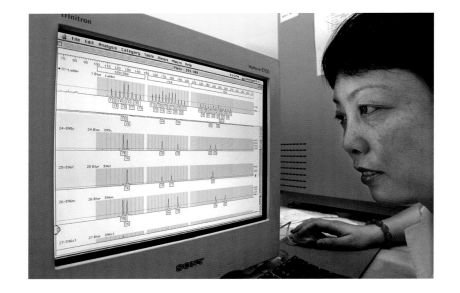

When technicians at the lab receive your container, they extract your DNA from the cotton swab, chewing gum, or mouthwash. They determine your DNA information and send you the results. They will also put your results online, with a username and password that only you know.

If you are a match with another customer, you can choose to be contacted. On the 12-marker test, if you get a match, it does not necessarily mean you are cousins. If, however, you have the same last name *and* a DNA match, then it's highly likely that you are related.

DNA testing labs will usually store your DNA in case you decide to have a more advanced test done later. Or, if you wish, you can ask them to destroy your DNA at any time.

The DNA that is collected cannot reveal whether you have particular diseases, and it cannot tell you whether you are likely to get a disease. The DNA can't be used for cloning or any other purpose.

Above: Current genealogy work is displayed on a home computer. Today, many people use modern equipment and DNA testing to link family trees.

DNA Testing in Genetic Genealogy

Above: The DNA test for males examines the Y-chromosome. Fathers pass this Y-chromosome unchanged to their sons.

There are two kinds of DNA tests for genetic genealogy. One test is for males, and the other is for females.

The DNA test for males examines the Y-chromosome. Only males have a Y-chromosome. It is responsible for the male gender. Fathers pass this Y-chromosome unchanged to their sons. Sometimes this test is called the paternity ancestry test, or Y-line DNA test. A father and a son will have the same Y-chromosome on the DNA test. A man's father will have the same Y-chromosome results as that man's son.

The other DNA test is usually conducted on females. It is called the mitochondrial DNA, or mtDNA, test. This test examines the DNA that is found in the mitochondria of cells. This kind of DNA is passed unchanged from mother to daughter. This mitochondrial DNA will be the same for the daughter, the mother, and the mother's mother. Sometimes this test is called the maternal ancestry test, because it can trace the mother's line. Sons also inherit the mitochondrial DNA from their mothers, but males don't pass it on to their children.

Above: The DNA test for females is called the mitochondrial DNA, or mtDNA, test.

Here's an example of how DNA testing could work for genealogy: Fred Rosenpurple from Los Angeles has been working on his genealogy. While searching the Internet, he finds another family of Rosenpurples in New York City. Since Rosenpurple is a very rare name, Fred wonders if they are related. He contacts them, and they compare genealogical notes. They can find no connection among their parents or grandparents. However, neither Rosenpurple family knows their great-grandparents. A male from the Los Angeles Rosenpurple family and a male from the New York Rosenpurple family both take Y-line DNA tests. When the results come back, the DNA tells them that they have a common ancestor. The two Rosenpurple men are long-lost cousins!

DNA tests cannot say which ancestor is common. Is it the great-grandfather? The great-great-grandfather? What the tests will provide are probabilities. For example, the report may state, "There is a 50 percent chance your common ancestor is 1 to 3 generations back, and a 95 percent chance your common ancestor is 1 to 10 generations back," or something similar.

Left: A DNA test cannot say which ancestor two people have in common, but it can provide probabilities.

Above: It's possible to use DNA testing to find a connection between distant relatives.

Deep Ancestry: When Genes Mutate

Above: DNA testing can look way back into human history.

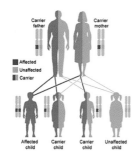

Above: Subtle changes in DNA may cause a gene mutation that is passed down to a person's descendants.

DNA testing can give us information about two things: our recent lineage and our "deep ancestry." Deep ancestry is a tool that looks way back into human history, back to the dawn of humanity.

DNA usually passes unchanged from father to son, and from mother to daughter. However, over the course of thousands of years, there will be subtle changes in the genes. For some reason, the DNA does not always copy itself exactly when it is passed from parent to child. When a gene changes, it is called a mutation. These mutations are usually minor, or even invisible to others.

When a gene mutation occurs, it is passed down to the descendants of the person with the mutated gene. The group of people who have the new, mutated gene are called a haplogroup. Eventually, someone from that group will have a mutation, and their descendants will form a new haplogroup. Scientists can track these haplogroups, like a trail of genetic breadcrumbs. This allows scientists to peer deep into our ancestry.

Above: When a gene mutation occurs, it is passed down to the descendants of the person with the mutated gene. The group of people with the new, mutated gene are called a haplogroup.

Deep Ancestry: Haplogroups

Above: A cave painting of natives from southern Africa. About 50,000 years ago, a group of people migrated out of Africa.

A DNA test can reveal your haplogroup. Haplogroup assignments are different for males (based on Y-chromosome) and females (based on mtDNA). Haplogroups look back many, many generations. Your haplogroup tells you the migration patterns of your ancient ancestors.

The current theory is that about 60,000 years ago, all humans lived in Africa. Then, about 50,000 years ago, one group of people migrated out of Africa. This haplogroup had a marker on the chromosome called M168. Some of the people from M168 went eastward, to populate Asia. Another haplogroup went north. The groups can be tracked by looking at how the DNA has changed and mutated over the years.

These migration patterns of your ancient ancestors are not exact. They say where populations of people went, not individuals. The test can't tell you where your direct ancestors lived. It only says that a majority of the people in this haplogroup populated a particular section of the world.

Above: The current theory is that about 60,000 years ago, all humans lived in Africa.

Over thousands of years, people left Africa to populate other areas of the world.

Tracing the mutations of the genes is the task of genetic genealogy's map of the human tree. Some of these mutations are invisible. Other mutations helped people survive in different parts of the world. Skin color, for example, is a mutation that helped people as they migrated north. Lighter skin helps the body absorb more vitamin D from the sun. This is important because people in northern latitudes live in shelters during the winter, and don't get as much sunlight as people living in sunny Africa.

Deep ancestry genetics have helped historians learn that the ancient ancestors of Native Americans lived in northern Mongolia. They spent several thousand years migrating across Beringia, a land bridge between Siberia and Alaska that is submerged today.

Because of deep ancestry DNA tests, historians know that the first inhabitants of Australia came from Southeast Asia about 50,000 years ago. Their haplogroup has a marker on the chromosome called M130.

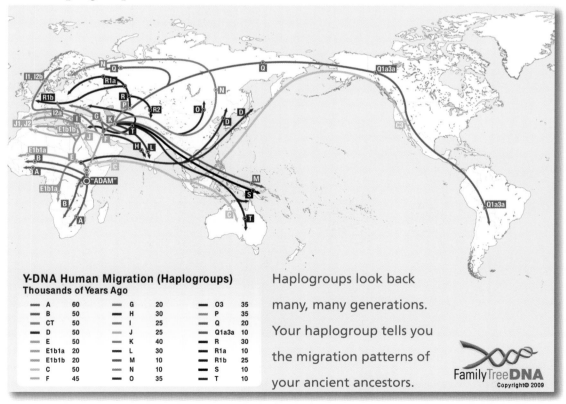

Y-DNA Human Migration (Haplogroups)
Thousands of Years Ago

A	60	G	20	O3	35		
B	50	H	30	P	35		
CT	50	I	25	Q	20		
D	50	J	25	Q1a3a	10		
E	50	K	40	R	30		
E1b1a	20	L	30	R1a	10		
E1b1b	20	M	10	R1b	25		
C	50	N	10	S	10		
F	45	O	35	T	10		

Haplogroups look back many, many generations. Your haplogroup tells you the migration patterns of your ancient ancestors.

FamilyTreeDNA
Copyright© 2009

Above: Tracing the mutations of genes is the job of genetic genealogy's map of the human tree. Skin color, for example, is a mutation that helped people survive in different parts of the world.

Your Genealogical Journey

Genealogy is hard work. DNA testing gives us one more tool to use to find our roots. DNA testing is never a substitute for the detective work of genealogy. We still need to look through censuses, find birth certificates, and talk with relatives. But DNA might help break through a brick wall or two. And as genetic tools advance, the future is bright for how it might help us understand where we came from. Whether we are talking about recent lineage or deep ancestry, we hold in our cells the information about our ancestors.

Genetic genealogy reminds us that we're all related somehow. No matter what our language, skin color, politics, or personality, we all come from the same place. Our ancient ancestors traveled together, ate together, and raised children together.

Above: Genetic genealogy reminds us that we're all related somehow. Our ancient ancestors traveled together, ate together, and raised children together.

Glossary

ANCESTORS

The people from whom you are directly descended. Usually this refers to people in generations prior to your grandparents.

CENSUS

The government's records that show information about who lives in this country and where they live. Also the process of collecting that information.

CHROMOSOME

A single piece of coiled DNA that is found in cells.

DNA

An organic chemical called deoxyribonucleic acid, which contains genetic information. It is often called the building block of life.

GENE

A sequence of DNA that gives the body information about various traits.

GENEALOGY

The study of your ancestors and your family history.

GENETIC GENEALOGY

The study of genealogy with the tools of DNA testing and genetic research.

HAPLOGROUP

The descendants of a single individual who first had a certain genetic mutation.

MIGRATION

When a group of people moves from one place to another.

MITOCHONDRIA

An organ structure within cells. DNA in mitochondria is passed from mother to daughter.

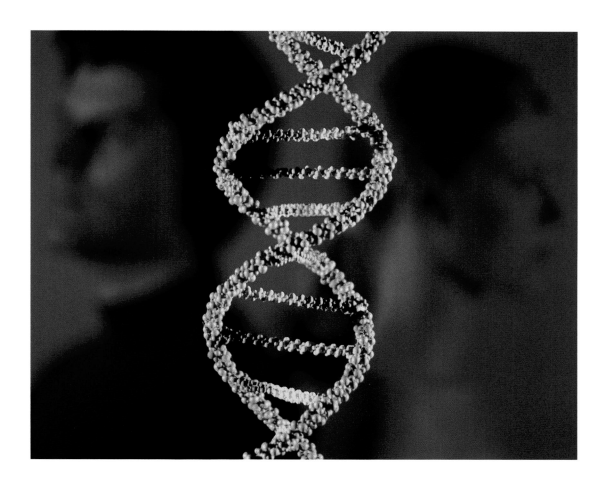

Index

A
Africa 24, 26
Alaska 26
ancient ancestors 24, 26, 28
Asia 24, 26
Australia 6, 26

B
Beringia 26

C
Caribbean Sea 6
Cheddar Gorge 8
Cheddar Man 8
chromosome 8, 12, 14, 18,
   24, 26
Columbus, Christopher 6
Columbus, Diego 6
Cook, James 6

D
deep ancestry 22, 26, 28
DNA testing 6, 8, 14, 16,
   18, 20, 22, 24, 26, 28
Dominican Republic 6

E
England 8

G
gene mutation 22, 26
genes 8, 10, 12, 22, 26
genetic genealogy 4, 18, 26,
   28
Gobi Desert 8

H
haplogroup 4, 22, 24, 26
Hawaii 6

I
Internet 20
Ireland 8

K
Kamehameha, King of
   Hawaii 6

L
Liqian 8
Los Angeles, CA 20

M
maternal ancestry test 18
migration 24
mitochondria 12, 18
mitochondrial DNA test 18
Mongolia 26
mtDNA test 18, 24

N
Native Americans 26
New York City, NY 20
Niall of the Nine Hostages 8
Noigiallach, Niall 8
nucleus (cell) 12

P
paternity ancestry test 18

R
Roman Empire 8
Rosenpurple, Fred 20

S
Scotland 8
Siberia 26
Somerset, England 8
Spain 6

Y
Y-chromosome 8, 18, 24
Y-line DNA test 18, 20

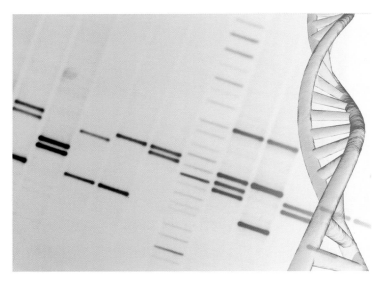